MEDIA COLLUSION

Journalism and Marketing Experts
Uncover the Secrets of:

- Sneaky Advertising
- Targeted Persuasion
- AI and Tracking
- Political Deception
- Dishonest News

PHILIP R. DUNN

FIRST EDITION

Media Collusion

ISBN: 978-1987594201

Printed in the United States of America

© 2018 Synapse Services Co.

Cover Design

Philip Ryder Dunn

Original Cover Artwork

Philip Ryder Dunn

Interior and Layout

Philip Ryder Dunn

Student Resources

Media-Collusion.org

Send inquiries to info@media-collusion.org

MEDIA COLLUSION

Journalism and Marketing Experts
Share the Secrets of:

 Sneaky Advertising

 Targeted Persuasion

 AI and Tracking

 Political Deception

 Dishonest News

PHILIP R. DUNN

FIRST EDITION

DEDICATION

To Mom, Dad, Ryder, Jameson, Charlotte and Lori for inspiring me and helping craft the ideas herein. Also to all the students who are changing their media outlooks by questioning the entire system.

Table of Contents

"If you don't read the newspaper you are uninformed, if you do read the newspaper you are misinformed."

— Mark Twain

How Strangers Manipulate You and How to Fight Back

Today's media landscape is shaping and confusing the minds of young people at warp speed. Even adults trained in critical thinking and academic analysis get confused with the incessant noise and suspect claims that flow freely across the multi-channel, multi-device media world.

One of the big problems is that advertising and persuasion mechanisms are baked right into the product, and it's now easier than ever to insert it, track it, retarget consumers and generally dupe people into misinformed positions in order to cultivate:

- Buying decisions
- Political decisions
- Medical decisions
- Financial decisions
- Lifestyle choices
- And other related drivers of everyday living and long-term planning

None of this is particularly new. It's just that the science of scamming, duping, cajoling and nudging is getting dangerously competent. Unfortunately, advertisers have taken wisdom from books like Robert Cialdini's *Persuasion* and turned it loose within the worlds of print journalism, TV, radio, podcasting and elsewhere. The upcoming generation of consumers is facing some of the smartest, most irresistible messaging techniques in history.

Smart companies view the media as hired storytellers to be manipulated on their behalf (many have always held this view, especially those in Public Relations or PR). Toms Shoes, the media-savvy shoe company founded in 2006, baked story into their product by giving away a pair of shoes for every pair they sold. That angle and philanthropic story helped them grow into a footwear giant. Willing media participants played a huge role in their success by covering the company's many PR successes with Toms-wearing celebrities, third world philanthropy and related events. Toms' success spurred hundreds of other companies, including the Gap, Pampers and Crocs, to copy their buy-one-give-one-away angle. Still other companies fool the media year after year with much less genuine stories (deceptive even).

> **What is a Public Relations or PR organization?**
>
> According to Wikipedia, PR is "the practice of managing the spread of information between an individual or an organization (such as a business, government agency, or a nonprofit organization) and the public. Public relations may include an organization or individual gaining exposure to their audiences using topics of public interest and news items that do not require direct payment."
>
> More on PR in Part 5.

If you Google Dawn dishwashing liquid and oil spill, you'll see more storytelling at work that gets picked up by the mainstream press and shared heavily on YouTube. You'll also see some controversy and irony about using petroleum based products like Dawn to clean up oil spills that affect wildlife.

Later, we'll show you how Toys R' Us and Target trot out the same story every holiday season, while local news stations consistently take the bait and provide glowing coverage.

Today, journalistically questionable and semi-bogus outfits like Buzzfeed, Vox and Vice rule content production, while technology behemoths like Apple, Google, Amazon and Facebook control advertising delivery methods. In years past, centralized juggernauts like the CBS Evening News, The Wall Street Journal, various magazine and radio conglomerates, CNN, the Los Angeles Times, NPR and even Pravda managed to guide public discourse with relative ease. They claimed to separate news from advertising with an impenetrable wall (in some newsrooms, it was an actual wall). Yet these publications, by their very nature, were PR channels. Large businesses, like professional sports teams, amphitheaters, movie studios, Fortune 500 companies, and similar concerns enjoyed steady coverage in exchange for pay-to-play advertising expenditures. Politicians used these old platforms to great effect, as well (and great expense).

In decades past, the editor influenced and controlled your "feed." Now you and your friends do to some extent. The platforms that control information presentation algorithms have a significant amount of control, as well (Facebook, Google, Amazon, Apple). We may soon see a day when actual headlines are customized based on your public profiles, fears, wants and individual quirks.

In order to navigate these new mine fields with some sanity, the best thing a student (young or old) can do is to get smart about how they're being manipulated and pitched.

Goals

> **"Do not seek the truth; only cease to cherish opinions."**
>
> **– Seng-ts'an**

Before you're finished with this book (and the course, if you're enrolled), it's useful to set some goals. So, how do you want to end up when this is complete? What's on the other side? How can you be transformed?

Here's a short list of reachable goals. By the time you're finished, you'll:

- Have the ability to analyze and combat advertising strategies and be intentional about your consumer choices
- Possess critical thinking skills that allow you to examine the motivations, economics and powers behind 1) Entertainment, 2) News and 3) Advertising media.
- Have the ability to lucidly debate and explain the modern media landscape
- Make better life decisions based on a clearer view of how the media world works

When we're talking about the "media world" for the purposes of this book, it's a larger animal than you might initially consider. From here on out when we say media, we're talking about the inter-connected entities and practices that include:

- Digital, print and broadcast publishers
- Social media platforms
- Public, private and non-profit influence groups
- Traditional advertising
- Native advertising
- Marketing

All these will be explained in context. As you see how they're connected, you'll be able to guide your life choices and make more aware, less emotionally driven decisions (decisions that are often crafted by people outside of your own intentions, aspirations and goals).

How To Use The Links In This Book

Within the pages that follow, you'll see images and links to articles, YouTube videos and audio.

To make it easier on you, we've provided shortened URLs (they're all safe), and keyword boxes that look like the following:

> JORDAN PETERSON
> YOUTUBE
> PROFESSOR
> RESPONSE

Talk or type these words into Google or Youtube on your phone, tablet, laptop or desktop, and you'll get right to the example. Easy.

All the links are available on the Media Collusion website, as well.

The PDF version of the text has the keyword boxes and clickable links throughout.

A Taste: Critical Insight for Understanding Political Advertising

"Disobedience is the true foundation of liberty. The obedient must be slaves."

– Henry David Thoreau

If you like the following analysis, you're going to get a lot out of this course and the text hereafter. We go deeper into these issues in Part 8, but the general overview of the issue follows.

The American political system, the news media and the advertising industry are symbiotic. Every two to four years – as election cycles in the country dictate – candidates raise large amounts of money, most of which is spent on advertising that's designed to persuade the public to vote them into power or solve some particular issue via proposition. This is a cycle:

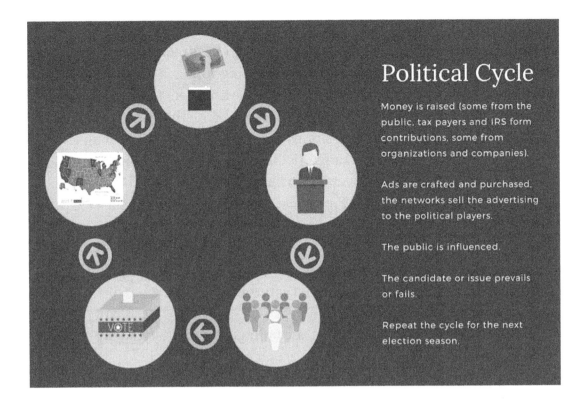

The biggest winners in this system are the large media publications and the cable news networks, national network news and local news stations. The various problems this arrangement causes should probably be looked at more closely and perhaps remedied.

One salient issue is that the political players, who can easily direct money into specific localities via network and local news ad buys, have come to ignore specific states and communities, because they've become irrelevant ad targets. In recent decades, California, for example, votes overwhelmingly Democratic in presidential elections. The candidates, in turn, have learned not to spend campaign and advertising dollars in the state, because it's money wasted on an assured outcome. States like Ohio, Pennsylvania and Florida, however, attract huge amounts of ad dollars because voting there is much more competitive. As a result, California news outlets don't get the same kind of cash infusion every two to four years as many other states.

Another recent complication is the internet. Social media platforms and the internet have – to the consternation of many – produced a wrinkle in the conventional cycle. Candidates and causes can go directly to voters and bypass the traditional advertising and publishing routes.

This does not sit well with advertisers or the news outlets that run the ads and cash the ad buy checks. If a candidate can go directly to the people via Twitter to promote her causes, positions and interests, then almost all parties connected to the traditional advertising system lose out. This includes agencies, creatives, ad buyers, distribution and the traditional networks. This is an evolving issue for the news industry, social media companies, and the candidates and propositions. Some questions:

- How much of a typical campaign ad budget has been usurped by Facebook, Google, Twitter and other internet advertising campaigns?
- How much money is not spent on ads because candidates can do direct to the people?
- Can mainstream media prevent the encroachment of social media and claw back ad dollars?
- Do traditional networks demonize social networks in their reporting and entertainment coverage in order to stay relevant?
- When are platforms like Facebook and YouTube considered TV networks as opposed to a social networks?

Developments surrounding hacks, data breaches, click bots, click farms and compromised social networks confound the issue further. If Facebook is partly responsible for election outcomes, then how should their influence be monitored, regulated or otherwise policed (if at all)? Is this a free speech issue or an equal access issue like TV equal time political coverage laws governed by the Federal Communications Commission (FCC)?

We'll explore these issues and the complex inter-dependencies of modern news, entertainment and advertising in the pages that follow.

Part 1 – Historical Perspective and Analysis

"If the path before you is clear, you're probably on someone else's."

– Carl Jung

We're going to move quickly through this section, because it's covered well elsewhere, and you've probably visited some of these topics in history and writing classes.

We'll start with Gutenberg. In the mid-15th century A.D., efficient printing came into widespread use because of Gutenberg's movable metal type and the use of paper mills that were typically driven by river power. Cheap, available paper and this efficient way of using metal letter and punctuation pieces and new oil inks made durable, legible, highly-efficient printing of books possible. This allowed the widespread dissemination of information (starting with bibles in Western Europe). This was a big advancement over traditional scroll paper and pen-scribe hand lettering. With a Gutenberg press, you could set up the pages of a book by typesetting and then print off hundreds of pages at a time. It was great for flyers, announcements, posters, pamphlets, newspapers and actual books. Eyeglass technology and widespread literacy helped, as well.

The production and distribution of books and periodicals continued to snowball and spread throughout the world through the coming centuries, only to be replaced by digital desktop publishing in the late 1970's to mid-1980's. Some publishers still use traditional typesetting based on the Gutenberg technology.

So, printing led to the production of all kinds of information dissemination. Here are just a few of the popular formats:

- Fiction books
- Non-fiction books
- Almanacs
- Newspapers
- Poster boards & announcements
- Billboards
- Pamphlets
- Political brochures and flyers
- Religious documents
- "How to" writings
- Advertising of all kinds
- Manuals and instructions
- Propaganda pieces

Almost all of these formats translated to radio when it was invented and its use spread in the early 20th century. Telephone and telegraph technology preceded radio in the 19th century. Telegraphy was primarily used for transmitting messages over an electrical wire or long wave radio, as in trans-Atlantic or ship to shore communications. These communications could be considered similar to the short message formats of today's texting or emails.

Early on, radio communications emulated telegraph and telephone communications, but the radio we typically associate with news and entertainment (and eventually TV) is what we're talking about the longer format communications in the bullets above. This is "media" radio for our purposes. Broadcast radio's heyday spanned from the 1920's (AM radio) to the development of FM radio in the 1930's and popular radio usage throughout the 40's and 50's and up until today. It was used for war propaganda during the major wars of the 20th century. Of course, music, talk shows, political programming, weather and crop reports, and all kinds of other programming uses were available over the decades.

Simultaneous to radio, photography and moving pictures captured on film to tell stories emerged around the turn of the 20th century. Newsreels were employed to relay war and propaganda news to U.S. and European audiences during the World Wars. They were typically played before movies started in theaters.

This media transformed into television in the 1950's. Black and white TV was available in the U.S. and Britain after World War II, and color TV became widespread in the mid 1960's.

These technologies are all deemed "additive," meaning that none of them replaced or significantly displaced their precedent. People used them as we do today. We read newspapers, books, and other texts, and additively, we listen to audio and view films and videos in various digital and non-digital formats (including good old-fashioned radio). Wireless internet connectivity is a form of radio, actually.

Recent Media History - Transitional Times

> **"In times of change, learners inherit the earth, while the learned find themselves beautifully equipped to deal with a world that no longer exists."**
>
> **– Eric Hoffer**

If you were born between 1930 and 2000, you were forced to deal with some of the most striking media changes known to any generation that preceded it.

Some of this change had to do with technological, tool or equipment changes. I was born in 1968. My parents typed on manual typewriters when they were growing up – you know, the kind with the lever mechanisms that strike with a beautiful snappy micro-thud. They dictated notes to cassette tapes that were transcribed by secretaries and transcription services.

I typed on an IBM Selectric typewriter that had a wonderful spinning ball in it that was fast at punching up the characters. Most of my classmates used these throughout the late 70's and early 80's.

I got my first computer when I was 9, because my dad was an early PC programmer. This was 1977. The computer was the Apple II+, which was the 2nd generation, basically, one removed from the garage-hacker Apple I.

If you were born past 1988, you probably don't remember much about times without the internet, which came into widespread prominence in 1992-1993 with the Mosaic browser (or earlier if you had access to academic labs).

Word processing with something like Microsoft Word or Wordstar (throwback) was still very similar to throwing a piece of paper into a typewriter, adjusting the margins and then hammering out the document. Spell check and cut & paste, however, brought things to a whole new level. You could sprint with a document then edit it later without having to stop and correct things with Liquid Paper. Digital cut & paste made editing and reworking documents even easier (this feature would gain even more significance when the web opened up a world of other resources).

Pre-internet research involved going to libraries and looking things up in physical books, then getting that information into a word processing document manually. It was time consuming to say the least, and we didn't have access to "global search." I'm not talking about search engine searches yet. Global search was a concept that came out of early CD-ROMs. These were the pre-DVD discs that typically held 700MB of data. Almost a Gigabyte. Encyclopedia-style publishers put all kinds of reference materials onto CD-ROMs and later read/write DVDs. The idea that you could search a huge volume of texts and images with a keyword was the big breakthrough.

Simultaneously, the young internet was emerging along with its ability to search articles, documents and other academic archives via tools like AltaVista, Excite, Infoseek, Ask Jeeves and Yahoo!. Google (and later Bing) would replace all of those.

These days, important search technology developments are happening around helper devices like the Amazon Echo, Google Home, Siri and Google Now. Interestingly, since the commercialization of the web, which started in the mid to late 1990's, another important search tool has come into prominence – Amazon. If anyone is searching for a product these days, they often skip Google and head straight to Amazon, since Amazon carries almost every product in the world, and Amazon Prime members can get products shipped free with their subscription to the service. This is a problem for Google. Alexa voice search and Google Home's "ok Google" functions are becoming critically competitive.

The commercialization of the web, by the way, took slowly and now allows everyone to find, order and get products delivered via phone, tablet and desktop browser. This wasn't always the way it was, and it took a long time for people to get used to trusting e-commerce sites with their credit card or banking info. E-Commerce sites also took quite a long time to get to their current level of competency and ease-of-use. Some still suck, but it's generally easy for anyone with some simple web development skills to set up a highly usable shopping cart system and e-commerce site. It took roughly 20 years to get us to this trusted online shopping state.

Google's YouTube needs to be discussed, as well. It's the #2 "search engine" in the world behind Google. More and more, people start their web searches with YouTube, and while it's technically not a web search engine, we often treat it as such. This is especially the case when we're looking for ways to do things (like cook, solve software problems, or figure out features in programs like Photoshop) and when we're looking for entertaining, funny or newsworthy videos that we've heard about. People look for product reviews and product comparisons on YouTube, as well. It's not really searching the whole web, but it could be argued that it's searching *almost* the entire web of video content. By the way, "according to a report by Defy Media, about 63% of millennials would try a product or brand recommended by a YouTube personality, compared to 48% who said the same about a TV or movie star." (Fortune Magazine, April 18, 2018)

So, what does all this have to do with media? Why are media and commerce so tightly linked?

If you look at the history of advertising, it evolved as a media-product partnership. Most general media publications like newspapers and magazines, financed their operations with advertising. This included radio and TV programming, which historically were a little different than print publications. We'll get into more of that later when we discuss the FCC and broadcast licensing. Also, when we mention internet publications here, we're now talking about everything, including YouTube channels, blogs, SoundCloud pages, Instagram accounts, Facebook pages, subscription sites, and on and on. Some of these are financed by advertising, some are funded by donations and subscriptions, and some are totally free and ad-free. The free ones are often supported by non-governmental organizations (NGOs) and other types of non-profit organizations. Examples of these include the Ford Foundation, the Bill and Melinda Gates Foundation, the Rockefeller Foundation, the American Red Cross, Planned Parenthood, MoveOn.org, and United States Agency for International Development (USAID).

Now, with the internet, commercial interests and digital publications (everything web) are even more tightly integrated and more loosely policed. Back in the days of regionally monopolistic newspaper publications, for example, editors went to great pains to separate what was reported in the publication from what the advertisers were doing (sometimes compared to the separation of church and state). This line blurred when specialty and trade magazines started to tie article content to advertiser interests. You see this quite often in community magazines that promote local shopping, food, entertainment and other lifestyle articles. There's a known "pay-to-play" model where advertisers get editorial coverage when they purchase ads. It's part of the ad buy package. Sophisticated, serious newspapers didn't do this, but the magazines went all in on this trend. It was a great way to make a local publication profitable while promoting local businesses. My first introduction to this was when I was writing a business column for a local Orange County, California magazine called *Coast Magazine*. The job was to go out and interview local businesses then write up cute stories about them for the Bizz Buzz column. Each business that advertised in the magazine was granted one Bizz Buzz interview and publication. That's paid editorial. You get a perk – a snappy ego-column focused around the business's owner written by a budding journalist – thrown in with your expensive ad buy.

It's a bit disingenuous for the readers, however. When I wrote the column, I reviewed the business in glowing terms. Same with the restaurant and gallery reviews. They were all paid advertisers, so there was no way a negative comment or tip was ever going to make it into those pages. The original owner of that magazine had a philosophy, by the way, which fit very nicely with the business model: *If you don't have something good to say, don't print it.*

Let's backtrack a little bit and talk more about the recent history of publishing technology. When we talked about the Gutenberg press, we mentioned how difficult and time consuming it was to set type, deal with ink and print documents in large quantities. When Apple was a young company, they created a computer called the Lisa which would eventually evolve into the MacIntosh. The first Mac computers were a breakthrough for the publishing world. Those computers offered users fonts, typesetting tools, and layout tools in digital form – making previous physical layout and design practices obsolete. The term used for this was "desktop publishing," where the term desktop meant desktop computer or PC. If you're interested in printing, there were all kinds of other developments along the way, like photocopying and mimeographing, that you can look into. Wikipedia has a great entry on all of it:
https://en.wikipedia.org/wiki/History_of_printing

So, the Apple Macintosh computer could be considered the first chink in the armor of the traditional publishing model. That model includes radio, TV, theater and Internet. The "democratization of publishing" enabled via desktop publishing would evolve along a hockey stick graph as computers, printers, storage devices, software, cameras, cell phones, and networking (eventually the Internet) evolved.

Here's how it looks:

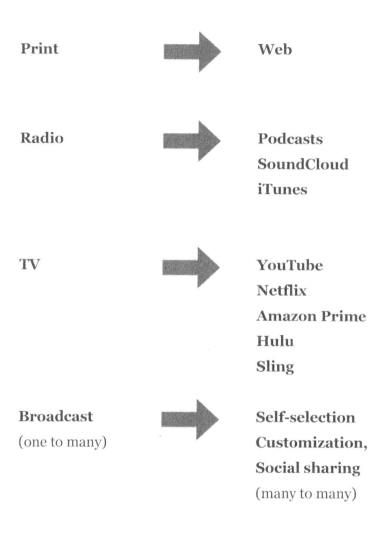

Print	➡	**Web**
Radio	➡	**Podcasts** **SoundCloud** **iTunes**
TV	➡	**YouTube** **Netflix** **Amazon Prime** **Hulu** **Sling**
Broadcast (one to many)	➡	**Self-selection** **Customization,** **Social sharing** (many to many)

Nothing changed about the human experience itself. We still have the same senses and skills required to view all this new content. We're readers, watchers and listeners. But the delivery systems and availability of content changed. With the many to many model of the internet, choice increased along with the number of voices, the intensity and crudeness of ideas, the effect of virality, and a whole host of other unintended consequences. The very interactivity of web discourse allowed the viewer to participate in the TV show to some degree. Comment posts and live discussion involved audiences over the network.

One interesting outgrowth of this phenomenon was how the practice of "trolling" so common on the internet made its way into old school programming like local broadcast newscasts (Trolls criticize, disrupt and generally bad-mouth posts and other comment threads online). You can see all kinds of broadcast troll videos on YouTube. A lot of them involve breaking into live broadcasts with vulgar or sexually explicit outbursts on camera. This kind of behavior wasn't previously common, and it was likely not considered civilized or appropriate for public display. Internet trolling practices paved the way for it, however, and the internet's archiving of the events encouraged them even more. It was quite a remarkable thing to behold.

So, what has changed? What's the difference between the old and new formats?

Traditional Broadcast & Publishing	Internet
Audience/readers have no commenting control (outside letters to editor pages).	Audience participates in the message via direct feedback/commenting and click, share, like, retweet popularity signaling. Sentiment signaling is also tracked via various web tools.
Large corporate organization develops and manages content development. This takes lots of time, preparation, research and expensive equipment and staff.	A mix of large, medium, small and micro-entities right down to an individual with a camera in a basement who produces content, sometimes spontaneously.
Entities are directly connected with and	Publishers often don't know who is

responsible for what kinds of advertising they publish and allow. Sales teams have direct relationships with the advertisers. Ads are often created by publishers, as well. They have the design teams available, for example, to develop ads for businesses.	advertising on their pages and in what specific geographies and markets. Google actually controls this. E.g. some major publications had to pull Google ads because they realized way too late that Google was running ads counter to their editorial policies on web pages and YouTube channels.
Advertisers have influence over programming (direct and indirect).	Advertisers have influence over where their ads show up based on keyword, demographic and geographic data. Psychographic data also come into play. Advertisers can pick what kind of person they want their ad to be placed in front of. There's also some thinking that they can pick what state of mind that person is in. The Facebook and Google models drive this. Advertisers may or may not know or realize where their ads are running, especially when they're doing large ad buys that span the web (banner ads, display ads, sidebars, etc.).
Publishers guard and inflate subscription numbers and viewership/listener confirmation is difficult to track and validate (Nielsen ratings). Stacks of magazines go unread at coffee shops, for example.	Bots and click farms give false impressions of the popularity of specific content and the ads within. A **bot** is a script or computer program that automates human behaviors across the web (clicks, likes, re-Tweets, etc.). A **click farm** is a group of people on computers that manually does the same things a bot does.

Advertising displays at "point of sale" (POS), on billboards, in relevant contexts (at a baseball game, for example), on buses, in the sky, wrapped around automobiles, in products (cereal), in meals (Happy Meals), in movies and TV shows (product placement), and more.

Web and mobile ads display in relation to contextual changes. Advertisers can buy targeted ads and/or "push" ads that appear when specific behaviors or geographical events transpire on mobile networks - in a mobile Facebook feed or another installed phone app. Amazon can show an ad when a person is at a Best Buy, for example. Geofencing is the name for this concept. Ads also follow you around the web based on products and topics you've looked at. This doesn't always work well. You're sometimes hit with ads about something you've already purchased.

Exercise: Screenshot and send me a page that shows advertising within a web article or mobile app that contains news (Facebook or Instagram). We'll discuss these in class and consider if or how they're targeting the advertising based on the content of the article or post/story.

Old School WOM and Your "Friends" As Sales People

"Arouse in the other person an eager want."

– Dale Carnegie

In the world without internet, there were these things called gossip and "word of mouth." This still goes on, of course. You'll see word of mouth abbreviated as WOM these days. The interesting thing about WOM and gossip is that it's limited in a non-internet world.

Your grandma might go to a butcher to pick up some

The Soap Opera

The style of TV show called a soap opera, which typically runs during the noon to 3pm hours of the day, was invented by soap manufacturers to influence stay at home moms in their purchasing decisions for things like laundry and dish washing detergents. They were hugely popular in the 1950's, 60's, 70's and 80's. The shows targeted women of a certain age that were involved in tasks of a certain kind (raising kids, maintaining a house, etc.). Eventually there were also night time soaps. You could say that some of this evolved into what's considered reality TV (with shows like *OC Housewives*). The shows typically focus on relationships and the dramas around those relationships.

steaks then run into a friend or two around town and tell them how great her butcher is. That kind of recommendation might allow word about the butcher to spread into a WOM universe capped by the number of people in the community or the surrounding areas. The same would apply to news about some known character in the community, gossip and bullying about someone, news of an upcoming event and so on.

Nowadays, however, information and news about products, people, events and more goes viral online and spreads way beyond the initial communities or friend groups where they originate.

It really started with email. Email did and still does allow you to copy people on the email and forward messages to groups of contacts. Those get forwarded on, and so on. You'll see this with popular joke and meme emails that go around. The same ones that make the rounds on email (or were famously viral in days past) may even show up as memes on social media platforms like Facebook, Instagram, Snapchat, Pinterest and Twitter.

The point here is that WOM can be launched to a whole new level with digital virality. This is way different than a few people in a small community talking about the newspaper around a coffee shop table. Exponential broadcasting effects can now happen among distinct groups of people with specific interests.

By the way, advertisers know that WOM is the most compelling form of recommendation. Back in the day, one mom recommending Tide for

meme

mēm/

noun

an element of a culture or system of behavior that may be considered to be passed from one individual to another by nongenetic means, especially imitation.

a humorous image, video, piece of text, etc., that is copied (often with slight variations) and spread rapidly by Internet users.

getting out tough stains (actually an army of moms across many communities) was far more valuable than a spot on the evening news. It's why reviews and stars are so important online. People want to hear from like-minded shoppers (and in many cases from their friends – think about clothing and rock concerts) about what they should buy. This applies to everything from foods and supplements to books and movies.

Some "friends" are even selling to each other. Experts sell classes and courses to each other. Hobbyist moms sell Etsy jewelry to their friends. Physical fitness buffs sell each other supplements, workout tools and paleo diet books.

In the chapters ahead, when we're talking about news, "fake news" and pap, we'll want to keep all these concepts in mind. First, let's get into some news basics to understand the old ways news was divided and how those lines are blurring in the digital age.

Exercise: Find two examples of WOM experiences you've seen online. Pick one that's a large meme or trend. Pick one that's very local and specific to your friend group. Take a screenshot or forward them to me via email. Include a short description of why you think this particular example can be considered word of mouth. Where do you think it started? Who started it? Is it driven by a person you know or do you think a company started it? We'll go over these in class.

Understanding "News" Basics

> **"Men are disturbed not by the things that happen, but by their opinion of the things that happen."**
>
> **– Epictetus**

When you watch a news show on TV, browse through a physical newspaper, click through a site like the Huffington Post, or bounce around YouTube for news videos linked to specific events, you're consuming all kinds of different publications that we generically describe as "news."

Every publication, however, has a mix of different news types. These fall into just a few different categories.

The first one is pretty simple – hard news. When there's a fire and a reporter takes down the facts of the incident, that's hard news. The reporter is responsible for describing the Who, What, Where, When and How of the event. If the reporter strays into more of the How and Why of the event, tracing those facts to issues outside of the specific event, then you're getting into opinion or analysis.

Opinion is usually identified as such by the publication and lives on pages marked Opinion or Editorial. Some news shows are all opinion, and they place that filter on the news of the day. Examples include Rachel Maddow (MSNBC) and Sean Hannity (Fox News).

Analysis is similar to opinion, but it's usually accomplished by sourcing and citing experts in a particular field, like climatology or politics. Opinion shows on TV usually bring in CIA experts to analyze worldwide events, or they bring in specific science experts to put a news analysis filter on developments in the environment, with food and whatever else is the hot topic of the day. This allows the host of the show or writer of the article to appear objective in their line of questioning. They can craft questions and answers by interviewing the analyst subject. The end result is often more opinion. This is very common these days on liberal or conservative news opinion shows. It's painfully obvious that they've brought in two "experts" on a particular subject, but the experts are in total agreement on the topic, and there's no effort to insert a third or balanced viewpoint. Ideally, you'd have the moderator/show host/writer interview two experts that have differing views and can articulate them well.

Unfortunately, biased opinion programs will cherry pick their guests to either be totally one-sided, or they'll pit a very articulate person who shares their opinion against a poorly skilled opponent who defends the other side of the issue. Both cases are common on Fox News, CNN, MSNBC and PBS Newshour. While news analysis tries to appear objective, it's often colored by the opinions and orientation of the particular news outlet. Analysis tries to ask why in very detailed ways in order to make sense of a topic or event.

When a TV opinion program has their talking head produce a monologue (usually at the beginning of the show), this is similar to an Op/Ed article in a print publication. There's one voice and opinion, and they craft a singular argument without using expert input. They may cite facts and expert quotes within the monologue or article, but the piece is generally guided by their own thoughts on the subject.

Baseball scores are hard news, but the coverage of the team is a little more subjective. The reason you get recaps and summaries of game performances is because the local publication has a contract or compact with the team to promote them. That's editorially selective. My local newspaper – the Orange County Register, for example – decides that they'll promote the Angels baseball team, and in return they get access to players and special events, the team places ads in their publication, and both companies collaborate on dozens of on-season and off-season promotions benefiting each business in a complementary way. They're partners, essentially. The scores and stats are hard news facts, but the arrangement with the team is something altogether different. The team didn't just buy an ad and expect a little quid pro quo. They work with the paper to develop the paper's "product" while benefiting from the Register's large sports fan audience.

Movie showtime schedules are hard news, but the arrangement between the publication and the theaters and movie studios is more subtly nuanced. Those theaters and studios purchase ads that run in the publication, and the publication writes reviews of those same movies. There's supposed to be an editorial separation between the advertiser and the influence of the reviewer, but that's not always so black and white. Some release events, like the Star Wars movie roll-outs, are so expensive and influential that editorial decisions are inevitably made to favorably review the movies, the events surrounding them, and the descriptions of all things related to the movies. Promotion also reaches fever pitch when a local team makes it deep into the playoffs or makes it to a championship.

Exercise: Send me two examples of "news" – one that's hard news and another that's analysis or opinion. You can use your phone to record it from the TV then email that short video file. You don't need to get the entire clip, just a snippet of a few seconds so we can hear the thoughts of the person or the facts being reported. Tell us why it's hard news or opinion in the body of the email. If you're forwarding a link to a written article, include a description of why you think it's hard news or opinion.

Photographs, Video Clips and Headlines

"Make promises. List benefits. Create attractive images."

– Marketing mantra

To the casual news observer, the news is a compilation of facts that are delivered directly to us via paper, screen, browser and TV. This couldn't be further from the truth. News events happen, and they're reported. However, they're passed through a fascinating filter before they reach us – humans! Yes, the news is edited and shaped by humans. They're editors, program directors and publishers. They're media executives that meet in fancy New York clubs and Washington D.C. lounges. They have agendas and personal biases. They're human, they make mistakes, and they advocate certain outcomes. This is especially relevant and more blatantly obvious on the news analysis side of things. But it creeps into the "hard news," too.

Remember, advertisers and PR companies affect this editorial process, as well. They show up more often in the "soft news," but they can creep into the hard news, especially when it comes to food, health and diet issues.

So how does this typically happen? We can start to examine the phenomenon by looking at photography, video clip and headline choices. These are editorial decisions made by living, breathing media experts.

Let's look at the common headline.

Headlines are chosen by editors, and they're prone to biases, opinions, worldviews, and the editorial guidelines of their publications. (By the way, in most large publications, editors choose the headlines after they're written by copy editors who've reviewed the original reporter's work.) You can take the same event and compare headlines from two different publications and begin to see different stories emerging. It's not so easy to do it with hard news, but it even crops up there at times.

Take a look at the following headlines, and you'll see the difference between detailed facts and hazy interpretation:

Judge Allows Testimony of Another Accuser in Cosby Case

By GRAHAM BOWLEY   FEB. 24, 2017

Bill Cosby arriving at Montgomery County Court in Pennsylvania earlier this month.
Andrew Renneisen for The New York Times

Bill Cosby Sex Assault Trial: Judge Allows Only 1 Other Accuser to Testify, Not 13

Prosecutors wanted to call more women to the stand

Joe Otterson, provided by

THE **WRAP** Covering Hollywood Published 9:01 am, Friday, February 24, 2017

   If you're only reading headlines, the meaning of these two headlines differs greatly.

   Where the headline appears is also important. Above the fold is an important concept here (see sidebar). Editors choose what goes on the front page of a magazine, newspaper or a website. They choose the size of the font, the number of words, the subheading or "deck" and a number of other subjective aspects that have to do with wording and their publication's particular style guide. As you know, what's on page one gets read by most, and what's on page 20 or at the bottom of the scroll is read only by the news fanatics that have way too much time on their hands. Search engines play a role in this, as well. News that's more popular (and clicked on more) bubbles up to the top of feeds like Google News, Yahoo News and in the Facebook news sidebar.

A book store owner has a similar power. Even though there are lots of diverse and interesting ideas within the books of her store, she has the power to decide which books are by the front door, which ones get big splashy displays, and which ones are stuffed on the shelves at the back of the store and in the corners where no one but book miners can find them. The book store owner has the prerogative to put the philosophies, stories, opinions and interests that she thinks the public needs wherever she wants. That kind of selection is not insignificant. Of course, the store owner has to consider what sells. The economics of book selling is certainly part of the equation.

Consider, however, that metropolitan newspapers in our day are effectively monopolies. Many of them are owned by papers from other towns, as well. If you're the only game in town, you present stories any way you want and the public goes along. Now, the internet changes that, and we'll address this more in a later chapter. But, the major news outlets in the country (*Washington Post, New York Times, Los Angeles Times/Chicago Tribune* – same company owns these two) are all owned by either powerful companies or powerful and wealthy individuals. Jeff Bezos of Amazon owns the *Washington Post.* The Sulzberger family owns the majority of shares in the *New York Times* (the Sulzberger family has ruled the paper since 1896). And, Australian billionaire Rupert Murdoch owns the *Wall Street Journal.* With monopolies of this sort, editorial control can potentially trump economic forces. The same could be said of Rupert Murdoch's Fox News, and Fox Entertainment (TV news shows and other broadcast programming) and 21st Century Fox (movies).

So, headlines matter. And the people managing the headlines do have significant input. The stories you see are carefully chosen because:

- History and statistical analysis proves that people gravitate to them or they've been trained to gravitate to them
- Certain publications have interest in specific topics and agendas
- Governments (local, state and national)

- have interests and agendas
- Advertisers have interests and agendas
- Activists, non-profit organizations and non-governmental organizations have interests and agendas
- Companies that hire PR firms have interests and agendas
- Reporters, analysts and "talent" have interests and agendas

The point here is that what gets covered, what gets hyped, and what gets bigger font sizes and red typeface is a product of a complex system of interested parties, only one of which is that first bullet – *the people whom the stories are aimed at*. Remember, the editor makes the decisions, but the editor is well aware of all these other forces in play, and the editor knows who's signing his paychecks.

Above the Fold

What is meant by "above the fold?"

While a lot of our current news is consumed on phones and screens, there was a time when people had their morning coffee and rode trains with a newspaper in hand (see image below).

The front page covered the whole of the front once it was unfolded vertically. The stories above that horizontal fold line were considered "above the fold." They usually contained larger font sizes than any of the other stories in the paper and were selected by editors and publishers/owners as the most important stories of the day.

Most people who read papers were familiar with the stories of the day that landed in this area, and editors went to great lengths to ensure that those stories were the most important. You could consider above the fold stories equivalent to stories that have gone viral today, but that doesn't quite explain it.

Above the fold was curated by various editors and publishers across the country. The way Facebook manages their news feed might be considered similar. The old choices were human, however, as opposed to algorithmic (although Facebook uses a combination of human plus algos).

The Mythical Wall Between Editorial and Advertising

"Fear is freedom! Subjugation is liberation! Contradiction is truth! Those are the facts of this world! And you will all surrender to them, you pigs in human clothing!"

– Satsuki

There used to be a well-defined line that separated hard news and opinion from advertising. That line is now more blurred than ever. With so much content to consume and so many "news" outlets across dozens of aggregators and social media platforms, we're inundated, as consumers, with stories that could be news or might be veiled advertisements bought and paid for by advertisers.

There are so many legitimate-appearing news outlets in our midst, as well. Some look very official, and their articles follow formal journalistic presentation practices, but they're providing all kinds of suspect information that's driven by political, social, and commercial agendas. For these kinds of sites, publications, YouTube channels, Facebook pages, podcasts and whatever else, there isn't necessarily an editorial team in place. And if there is, you don't know what they're up to unless you do some serious digging (like a reporter) into tax filings, LinkedIn profiles, court documents and the like. Who's got time for that?! But when you see a great headline and click through, there's a reasonable chance you're going down a rabbit hole.

Without an editorial team and a significant legal and ethical apparatus in place, publications quickly slide into this area where "fact" promotes commerce and political agendas, while lobbyists, PR companies and smear artists steer the messages in hard reporting.

The metaphorical (and sometimes physical) wall between editorial and advertising was once considered sacred. If a reporter or journalist crossed the line, mixing advertising with news reporting, they'd get fined, slapped, fired or shamed out of their position (maybe not slapped). If an honest editor didn't protect his reporters from dubious sources, he'd be canned as well.

Legitimate publications allowed advertising, of course, but they worked very hard to make sure the advertisers didn't take over the place. They kept advertising out of the hard reporting as much as they could. If they reported a baseball score, of course, they'd be promoting the local team. But they weren't going to let McDonald's into the body of the hard news coverage – which they do today, by the way, with companies like Starbucks, Toys R' Us and McDonald's. We'll get into these specific examples later.

Just keep it in your mind that there used to be a time when ad-supported publications and broadcasters fiercely fought against advertiser involvement in editorial content. There are publications that attempt to fight the good fight these days, however the persuasive forces aligned against them frequently succeed in placing their advertising-based stories within their pages and programs. Some of those companies may be actual advertisers in the publications. Some may not be.

Ad Agencies Get Smart

"It has been found that the less an advertisement looks like an advertisement and the more it looks like an editorial, the more readers stop, look, and read."

— David Ogilvy

Eventually, advertising agencies figured out that if you made your print advertisement look like an article – not necessarily news but feature, review, lifestyle, food or similar – you could trick the reader into thinking they were reading something that was part of the paper. Sometimes this was subtle, and sometimes it was just casual and not overtly tricking the reader (as in the ad featured below). The old Mad Men ad agencies of the 1950's perfected the technique. You could even say Claude Hopkins started the editorial advertising trend decades prior to the Internet in the 1920's and 1930's. Read Hopkins' book *Scientific Advertising* if you're interested in this stuff. *Ogilvy on Advertising* is also **very good.**

David Ogilvy pounded the editorial/native-ad drum incessantly. He proved that ads designed to look like editorial pages gather far more readers than those that don't. Here's an example of the kind of ad he espoused (see below). It's got a nice, beautiful picture with people for visual interest. The copy looks like an article, and the headline draws you in with curiosity.

The Rolls-Royce Silver Cloud – $13,995

"At 60 miles an hour the loudest noise in this new Rolls-Royce comes from the electric clock"

What makes Rolls-Royce the best car in the world? "There is really no magic about it— it is merely patient attention to detail," says an eminent Rolls-Royce engineer.

1. "At 60 miles an hour the loudest noise comes from the electric clock," reports the Technical Editor of THE MOTOR. Three mufflers tune out sound frequencies—acoustically.

2. Every Rolls-Royce engine is run for seven hours at full throttle before installation, and each car is test-driven for hundreds of miles over varying road surfaces.

3. The Rolls-Royce is designed as an *owner-driven* car. It is eighteen inches shorter than the largest domestic cars.

4. The car has power steering, power brakes and automatic gear-shift. It is very easy to drive and to park. No chauffeur required.

5. The finished car spends a week in the final test-shop, being fine-tuned. Here it is subjected to 98 separate ordeals. For example, the engineers use a *stethoscope* to listen for axle-whine.

6. The Rolls-Royce is guaranteed for *three* years. With a new network of dealers and parts-depots from Coast to Coast, service is no problem.

7. The Rolls-Royce radiator has never changed, except that when Sir Henry Royce died in 1933 the monogram RR was changed from red to black.

8. The coachwork is given five coats of primer paint, and hand rubbed between each coat, before *nine* coats of finishing paint go on.

9. By moving a switch on the steering column, you can adjust the shock absorbers to suit road conditions.

10. A picnic table, veneered in French walnut, slides out from under the dash. Two more swing out behind the front seats.

11. You can get such optional extras as an Espresso coffee-making machine, a dictating machine, a bed, hot and cold water for washing, an electric razor or a telephone.

12. There are three separate systems of power brakes, two hydraulic and one mechanical. Damage to one system will not affect the others. The Rolls-Royce is a very *safe* car—and also a very *lively* car. It cruises serenely at eighty-five. Top speed is in excess of 100 m.p.h.

13. The Bentley is made by Rolls-Royce. Except for the radiators, they are identical motor cars, manufactured by the same engineers in the same works. People who feel diffident about driving a Rolls-Royce can buy a Bentley.

PRICE. The Rolls-Royce illustrated in this advertisement—f.o.b. principal ports of entry—costs **$13,995.**

If you would like the rewarding experience of driving a Rolls-Royce or Bentley, write or telephone to one of the dealers listed on the opposite page.

Rolls-Royce Inc., 10 Rockefeller Plaza, New York 20, N. Y., CIrcle 5-1144.

March 1959

The Ogilvy ad also has a numbered list, which is important. In today's internet world, you may notice that numbered articles and listed articles are very popular. They call them "listicles" in the publishing trade.

Ad men were in constant battle with the publication consumer, the page-flipper as it were. It was a behavior battle that plays out to this day on the web. If you're a page-flipper in a doctor's office flipping through *Esquire* magazine, *Look* or *Popular Science* (suspend reality for a bit and pretend it's 1955), you would have had a magazine strategy for getting through the fluff and into the articles quickly. Turn past the beginning where the large photo ads are packed in. Past the table of contents and into another batch of big one-page display ads. Then, yay, you reach the article you wanted and you settle in for a read.

Ogilvy and his crew, however, wanted to stop you with that beautiful Rolls Royce and what appeared to be some tantalizing facts about the ride. Later on, magazines and newspapers adopted a practice to reclaim the wall between this kind of advertising and editorial. They started placing subtle words at the tops of the pages that read "Advertising Supplement" or "Paid Advertisement." In chapters that follow, we'll talk about how this plays out on the web with companies like Outbrain and Taboola. These advertising companies use behavioral targeting to promote companies in editorial that looks like articles, slideshows, blog posts, photos or videos. Their content is dynamically inserted into major publications with the tag "Around the Web" or "Related Items" or "Recommended by Outbrain." You've probably seen them all over the web on sites like *Fortune, Fox News* and *The Huffington Post.*

What is a Listicle?

A listicle is a mash-up or combination of the words list and article. See the image below to get the gist. For whatever reason, the human mind loves lists, bullet points and organized numbered things. And, numbers in headlines have proven to draw in more readers. The numbers 7 (lucky), 8 (just a cool number that's infinity if you topple it), and 3 (the magic number) are all good for listicles. As are 10, 18, 88, 77, 13, 33, etc.

The listicle articles themselves are attractive to readers because they offer a recipe, or a prescription or plan for getting something done or learning something. They also give the reader some sense that it's going to be a quick lesson. With huge listicles, 20+ items, they're telegraphing much more intensive learning and time spent. But the lower numbered ones are definitely showing the reader how much time or attention they may need to invest in the article. If you titled something different – like say "An In-Depth Tome on the Vagaries of Kanye" – you obviously have something different to contend with. Listicles say, "Hey, I'm easy, I'm informative, come spend a teeny bit of your time with me!"

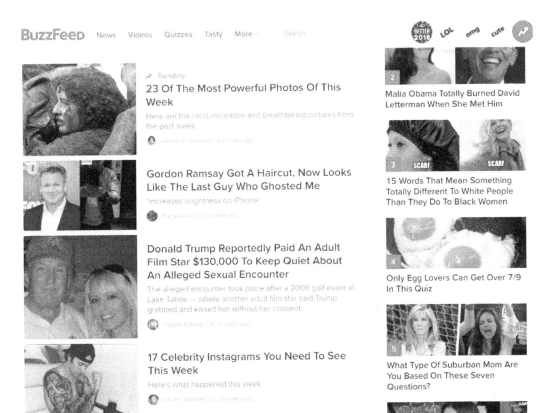

Part 2 – Media Motivation Mechanics

"The world is ruled and the destiny of civilization is established by the human emotions."

– Napoleon Hill

Offline and Online Persuasion

The types of persuasion you see on the web have been honed for decades offline. Formats include:

- Direct mail
- Magazines
- Flyers
- Posters
- Billboards
- Bus wraps
- Product placement
- Program sponsorship
- Speeches
- Public service announcements (PSAs)
- Church donation pitches
- Sky writing
- Grocery aisle ads
- Grocery floor ads
- Stickers
- T-shirts and clothing logos
- Equipment logos (skis, surfboards, boats, etc.)
- TV ads
- Infomercials
- Telephone marketing

The advertising receiving interface has always been the same – the human mind, body and spirit. The only thing that's really changed is the ad distribution interface. The web and our smart phones now deliver similar advertising. The effect is additive. You still see the other advertising. You just get more of it via your phones, smart watches,

Kindles, tablets, laptops and desktops.

The big difference between the old and the new is that Internet ads can be measured for exposure and performance by tracking cookies, pixel tracking and various other digital tracking methods that triangulate with external databases, GPS locations, app check-ins, and app push notifications.

There are also personalization factors in play. If you "like" certain bands, movies, personalities, clothing, brands, sodas, books, etc. via your social media accounts, you'll be delivered more of that stuff (and at opportune times and places if the marketing and advertising agencies are competent).

Email marketing plays a role, as well. When you sign up for notifications, you're enrolled in what are called drip campaigns or lead funnels. All kinds of web tools allow marketers to schedule evolving ad campaigns to your inbox. You've probably seen this before when you receive a welcome email. Then you get an offer. You might get a different offer at a later time based on what you did with the first offer. You could also get a free download, then get hit with an upgrade offer at another time. All kinds of different strategies and funnel tactics exist. Web sites also know when you return to your account. They'll hit you with a timely email if you've visited, for example.

A typical funnel looks like this:

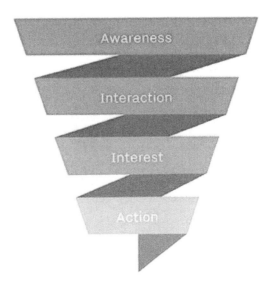

Sales Funnel

Awareness

Interaction

Interest

Action

What is "Newsjacking?"

In the early days of Twitter, Facebook and YouTube, the revered marketing and persuasion author David Meerman Scott coined the term for the practice of including popular, trending news stories into your content in order to gain keyword strength (SEO) and social shares. He called it *Newsjacking* and has a book by the same title that's still very relevant today. He wrote another one called *Marketing Lessons from the Grateful Dead* which is also fantastic. Required reading for marketers.

The popular examples used to describe successful newsjacking include Oreo's Super Bowl blackout and Kate Middleton baby tweets.

They're fairly self-explanatory =>

The approach is to take a highly popular event – the Super Bowl – and attach your brand to it. That one was fun, inventive and very much in the vein of classic newsjacking.

The royal baby example, which played out nicely across the social nets, is on the next page.

LONG LIVE THE CREME

These day, timing is critical for newsjacking. Everyone's now in on the game, and the best minds in advertising, humor and entertainment rev up their engines once fun, funny, popular, controversial news hits.

When the U.S. Supreme Court ruled on same sex marriage, Virgin Airlines newsjacked with this ad:

SAME SEX MARRIAGE BILL. PASSED.
Time for a honeymoon

Some newsjacking is pure product promotion (and questionable):

Did Hurricane Sandy affect your city? Get your generators, air mattresses & more in one place: spr.ly/6o18py14 #HurricaneSandy

← Reply ⟳ Retweet ★ Favorite

2
RETWEETS

6:05 PM - 26 Oct 12 · Embed this Tweet

Other posts are even more questionable. Thank you PETA:

Today, we honor Martin Luther King Jr. & the plight of animals who are tortured, abused & neglected: peta.vg/mlk #NeverBeSilent

7:17 AM - 20 Jan 2014

422 RETWEETS 117 FAVORITES

There's no use conflating two totally different topics in a tacky and offensive way. Marketers should know better. There have been a lot of these fails on MLK day.

Celebrity-jacking is newsjacking's close relative. With celebrity-jacking, the person, company or product that wants exposure attaches it's content to a specific famous celebrity or otherwise famous or infamous person.

Motivational business guru Charlie Houpert is notorious for the practice. Check out his YouTube page, and you'll see how all of his posts and titles attach celebrity names to whatever concept or topic he's covering:

3 Mindsets That Will Change Your Life

67K views • 2 days ago
CC

6 Types Of Charisma Women Find Irresistible

165K views • 1 week ago
CC

How To Crush Any Interview

59K views • 2 weeks ago

Elon Musk: How To Achieve 10x More Than Your Peers

189K views • 3 weeks ago
CC

The Best Charisma Breakdowns   PLAY ALL

Welcome to Charisma on Command where we talk about enhancing your charisma, confidence, and just be the better version of you! Learn how to be more charismatic and confident with

6 Types Of Charisma Women Find Irresistible

Charisma on Command ✓
165K views • 1 week ago
CC

The Dangerous Side Of Tom Cruise's Charisma

Charisma on Command ✓
479K views • 9 months ago
CC

The Infuriating Charisma of Gary Vaynerchuk

Charisma on Command ✓
106K views • 3 months ago
CC

How The Rock Went From Flop To Superstar

Charisma on Command ✓
134K views • 4 months ago
CC

His top videos jack Tim Ferris, the Marvel franchise, Elon Musk, Tom Cruise, Gary Vaynerchuk and Dwayne "The Rock" Johnson.

So why cover newsjacking and celebrity-jacking here? It's just good to become aware of how far brands, personal brands and influencers will go to get your attention. Newsjacking often comes off as clickbait, and the information beyond the fun image can frequently let you down. Content that relies heavily on newsjacking or celebrity-jacking often fails tests for depth, attribution, accuracy, usefulness and truthfulness. Otherwise, it's just plain fun. Proceed at your own risk.

Mob Mentality and Social Media

"People who are obsessed with appearance are the ones most likely to be fooled by it."

– anonymous

Much of the latest research on gender shows that boys and girls are equally aggressive - but boys play out their aggression more physically, and girls tend to play it out more socially. A good book on the subject for general (as opposed to academic) consumption is *Why Gender Matters* by Leonard Sax, M.D., Ph. D.

So what does this mean?

Boys and men will physically confront each other with threats of fights and actual fights. They'll usually engage in fairly violent sounding arguments, as well.

Females, on the other hand, often get involved in more intricate battles that play out via gossip, revenge and reputation sabotage. They'll align with groups of other females and play out acts of aggression with words, threats and suggested intent. The aftermath of male fights can be very short, and men will often become friends with their enemies faster than women. The results of men fights can be truly tragic – men are much more likely to be in prison for heinous acts of murder and physical violence. In contrast, the results of women fights can linger on for quite a while, but they're much less physically dangerous.

If you combine all that sociology with these digital screens we obsess over – some call them the black mirrors (after the Netflix Show of the same name) – you'll find additional sociological trends.

For example, if you give young boys an iPhone or an Xbox, most will be happy to play competitive games – some of which are violent, others not so much. It's virtualized fighting and score keeping similar to martial arts, warfare and sports competitions. That's where the boys are comfortable.

Give the girls black mirrors, and they'll eventually gravitate to social media platforms and group texting. They quickly figure out how to game social connections to discern pecking order, establish popularity, build bonds, help friends, marginalize enemies and so forth. Boys not so much. They'd rather blow up stuff via pixels.

The consequences of over-saturation with social media can be harmful to both genders, but it's been seen as especially harmful to females because they take to it so quickly. And, it's the nature of the beast. Social media is about real life in some ways – or it's about a "reality show" that's a little too close to home.

While the boys play in fantasy land, the girls are making very real connections and disconnections via virtual platforms. *And their effects can often be amplified to frightening degrees.*

One problem is that there's an unlimited downside of going viral on these social media platforms. Yes, you can go viral, blowing up and gaining overnight fame as a YouTube star (probably not, actually – there's really no such thing as overnight success, as you may have heard). But what about blowing up in the negative sense? What happens when five girls decide to screenshot and spread the negative comment or photo you posted on Snapchat with an audience of girls who will absolutely loathe it and spread it amongst their hater friends? That's a recipe that really can't be reproduced on Call of Duty or Fortnite (where the boys are). It's unique to Instagram, Snapchat, Facebook and God knows where else.

Basically, the upside to social media is fairly limited, while the downside is limitless. The perfect storm of rumor, innuendo, a bad photo and some trolls can spell D-I-S-A-S-T-E-R.

Plus, there all kinds of technically advanced image and video modifying apps out there these days. Ever heard of "deepfakes?" This is the AI-assisted face swapping software that can put any face onto another in a video. It was made famous by its Reddit following and its application in pornography. You could put a famous person's face onto a movie actress, and it looks real! Crazy stuff, and we certainly haven't seen the end of this. Although the Reddit group has been taken down, there are surely other outlets on the dark web for this kind of nonsense. It's made its way into politics, of course, with movies of Obama saying things he did not say. . . and it looks real.

Young people also get into trouble when they're expected to like something. There are instances (maybe you know of them) where groups of students will decide together whether or not to like or share certain updates from their peer groups. The assumption is that if they act like a group, they won't risk the embarrassment of being a black sheep on one of the posts that gets liked or shunned. Psychologically, it's fascinating, but for the kids within the tyranny, it's getting old, I'd guess.

Amplify all these ideas in the political realm, and you've got recipes for even more trouble. . .

- Doctored photos
- Fake stories
- Leaks from anonymous people who don't exist
- Deepfakes of candidates
- Audio mash-ups
- Audio fabrications
- Coverups and counter-coverups

There's no end in sight, really. Compounding the issues – Facebook is full of confirming opinions in the feed. Their algorithms promote content that people want to consume, and many people have friends and family that confirm their own beliefs. Some people have balanced political and ideological feeds and friends, but most trend toward homogeneity. Like people share like stories with like-minded people, and the beat goes on. Add in some falsified media or outright lies, and you've got a poked hornet's nest. Same with Twitter, of course, and anywhere else.

Some Advice for Future Online Stars

With the advent of Twitter, Facebook, YouTube, Instagram, LinkedIn and Snapchat and other social media platforms, there's been an interesting development.

Public figures and celebrities often feel compelled to comment on events, issues and other people publicly. Sometimes they have to (in the case of a public figure like a mayor or the President), but many times they just do (as with celebrities that think they're just smart or somehow more clever than the rest of us – remember these are teams of people working on the celebrity and political accounts).

The way social media works (and "newsjacking") is that you get exposure by piggybacking onto popular trends and scandals. So these people are incented to pipe up when things are going on – good, bad or indifferent.

Here's some advice if you ever find yourself powerful and influential: Make sure that whenever you're Tweeting you're acting as if someone from a magazine or newspaper called you up and wanted to interview you and get your take on the particular event or issue. It's that public, and the social media record doesn't really go away. It's probably pretty good advice for anyone, really. What you say now may come back to haunt you when you're famous . . or when you're taking the oath in court.

Making this one conceptual shift will save you a lot of pain. Loose lips make for embarrassing moments.

Exercise: List the most embarrassing – for the public figure – social media happenings this year. Who failed by posting too quickly and not thinking it through?

Silly Irony on Fox News

Here's another case study. One of the Fox News shows is hosted by Tucker Carlson, and he had a segment on April 5, 2018 called "Tech Tyranny." It's essentially a serial takedown of social media companies (which is currently in vogue after all kinds of data breaches and suggestions that Facebook may have lost Hillary Clinton the election in 2016).

In any case, the guest on the program was defending Facebook and technology companies in general against attacks that they're creating addictive products that make the lives of their users miserable. Tucker took the position that youth suicide rates have gone up and people are less satisfied with their lives because they're comparing themselves to others on social media sites. This topic has been explored in great detail for years, and there's some research to back it up.

My point here, however, is not to confirm or deny any of that. I just could not believe how the guest, Dean Garfield of an organization called the Information Technology Industry Council (ITI), couldn't defend against Carlson with one simple Occam's Razor argument. . . I'll spell it out here: Garfield missed a huge opportunity to counter Carlson's argument. Just like Facebook, Instagram and Snapchat, TV news shows are *designed* to be addictive. So are advertisements. TV is just a dumb one-way street (traditional old-school TV news without any immediate Twitter-like feedback). Like Facebook, cable companies also harvest and sell your information, which is a little smarter than broadcast TV. If this guy could have marshalled that one simple thought, he could have stopped Tucker Carlson in his tracks. All media is designed to gather the attention of the consumer and compel the consumer to take action based on persuasion tactics. That's the history of advertising! It isn't any different just because it happens to be occurring on Facebook, an admittedly smarter platform than a TV. It's just silly and unbelievable that Garfield couldn't connect the dots.

Here's the clip:

http://bit.ly/2qWeHYs

TECH
TYRANNY
DEFENSE

SEO and The Importance of Headlines, Titles, and Subjects

Headlines are now critical for what marketers and web analytics firms call SEO or search engine optimization. The practice and technology of SEO is a bit of a moving target, and there are multiple factors that influence

search en·gine op·ti·mi·za·tion
noun
COMPUTING
noun: **search engine optimization**;
plural noun: **search engine optimizations**
>the process of maximizing the number of visitors to a particular website by ensuring that the site appears high on the list of results returned by a search engine.

word choice for SEO. Ultimately the big search platforms make the rules about SEO, and SEO practitioners try to game them. That's been the history of it.

From Google's perspective, however, the core of SEO remains the same over the years. They want to offer the web searcher the best possible experience when searching for news, products, research information, images, podcasts, videos and so forth. If they can do that successfully, they can offer advertisers the best possible targeting and return on investment (ROI) on their ad campaigns. Ultimately, this SEO science comes down to *how humans think about subjects* and *what humans prefer to read or click on*. This applies to video and audio, as well, because you'll notice that every piece of media has tags, titles and descriptions. If you've ever produced a social media post, web page or YouTube post, you see that each particular instance requires that you either hashtag, meta tag, or title and describe your post (or some combination thereof). A meta tag is typically used in HTML on web page posts.

The whole SEO paradigm and Google's approach to indexing the web forever changed the "above the fold" issue we discussed earlier. News, for example, became less curated by editors and more "voted up" by search engine algorithms. Human curation does still exist on platforms like Facebook, Google News and elsewhere. There's also "crowdsourced" curation on platforms like Digg and Reddit.

Google and crowd sourced content's main indicator of a piece of content's relevance is how many other sites with high value on the same subject link to that piece of content. So, the content in an article, for example, has to be legitimate, thorough and blessed as the expert on the topic from the value and amount of inbound links.

Titles and headlines, however, help a great deal in getting this ball rolling. A headline is the major persuader in the mix. It forces the reader to decide whether or not to click on the link (description copy in the subheadings and description tags also contribute). The body copy determines how long the person stays on the link and whether or not other experts in the same area will link to the page.

That means there's lots of attention and science going into the evaluation and persuasion factors involved with titles, headlines and subheadings. The same research applies to email subject lines, by the way. Open rates, clicks and conversions are the metrics in email marketing, as opposed to impressions and inbound links in search.

Headlines, as in the BuzzFeed listicles we covered in Part 1, are intensely tested before they're used. Some of it is fluid, and publishers learn as they go, but many of the principles have been tested by previous generations of advertisers, advertorialists and native advertising experts.

The general point here is that headlines are designed to motivate web behaviors. That means they're designed to persuade and motivate people to get what they want out of them. If you're searching for "how to fix door lock on a 1998 Chevy pick-up," Google's job is to get you to the best information source on that topic. But if you're browsing news items and consuming media for entertainment or research, it's a little different. Media sites are constantly testing and perfecting what they present to you via titles and headlines. Yes, some people search for news information via search engines, but a lot of it is still unearthed via favorite sites and go-to media destinations. On top of all this, you can layer on social media and how information is shared based on popularity amongst friends *and how much a company is willing to pay for the advertising on the platform* (this includes Google AdWords, Facebook ads, Twitter ads, LinkedIn ads, Instagram ads and so on).

Is There Such a Thing as SEO for Social Networks?

SEO is not a practice limited to web pages. The same concepts apply to YouTube channels, Facebook pages and Instagram profiles. It's just a little different.

On Instagram, for example, what could be considered a "back link" would be the quality of the influencer that follows your profile. If I'm an artist and I have a business Instagram page that's focused on my original artwork, Instagram's influence algorithm likes me more if other highly-followed, highly-shared, highly-commented and highly-liked profiles in that same industry follow, like and comment on my posts. If I have influencer status, my posting is consistent, and I get a lot of likes and comments from common profiles and fans of my genre, then I'm much more likely to get on the Explore page, where I can gather up even more followers, likes and comments. It's a happy cycle.

There's a similar thing going on at Facebook. Their algorithm, however, works a little differently, and the goal for those who want to master the platform for business and exposure reasons is to more frequently and prominently get into the feeds of people who follow/friend you there.

Psychographics vs. Demographics

"The only good is knowledge and the only evil is ignorance."

– Socrates

When marketers talk about targeting specific people in their advertising, PR and influence campaigns, they'll typically use two different types of targeting approaches. The conventional (and older) form of targeting is called demographics. This is information about gender, age, marital status, location, and household income. Focus groups used to ask for this basic information before they led people through surveys about their buying habits, preferences and so forth. It's basic information that could allow a marketer to buy a list of people from a list broker with some general accuracy about what kind of neighborhood the person came from and how much they might be able to spend on a particular product. Credit bureaus and credit analysis firms like Experian, Equifax and Transunion would gather up this information, as well, and stockpile it in huge databases so they could make semi-accurate credit decisions about specific individuals.

Years ago, when most people in the U.S. purchased magazine subscriptions that were physically delivered to their homes (think Time,

Newsweek, Field & Stream, Cosmopolitan, People Magazine, The Economist, Sunset, Good Housekeeping, etc.), another layer of analysis was possible. They called it psychographics. This data could be meshed with demographic data in order to create an even better understanding of the consumer's potential buying potential. If they subscribed to Field & Stream, you could safely assume they might like fishing poles and off-road vehicles. If they subscribed to Good Housekeeping, you could assume they fit the psychological profile of a housewife. Buying decisions about cleaning products, interior design, family vehicles and food choices could be assumed and the appropriate advertising targeted to that person. Back in those days (think 1845 to 2000), the advertising was typically delivered via direct mail – postcards, letters and other types of color-printed mailers that pitched very specific products and services to these psychographic targets. E-Commerce had not taken off to any significant extent until post 2000.

In simple terms, demographics show the marketer who the buyer is, and psychographics tells the marketer why the buyer would buy something. The former is about generic profile, while the latter is about specific motivations.

Let's create a very basic buyer persona based upon what we know about the ideal customer for a nutritional counselor. Here goes!

From Wikipedia on "mail order":

"In 1845, Tiffany's Blue Book was the first mail-order catalogue in the United States. In 1872, Aaron Montgomery Ward of Chicago produced a mail-order catalogue for his Montgomery Ward mail order business."

"Color photography made its appearance in magazine advertising in the 1890s through the process of chromolithography," Banta writes. "Advances in the technology came in 1910, with the development of two- and three-color printing processes."

With the internet, advertisers and companies like Facebook and Google are able to make psychographics even more granular in their specificity. As you like bits of information on the web and share information about your life and preferences, these platforms learn details about you which they can share with advertisers. Here's the difference, showing typical data fields these platforms collect:

Demographics:

- Female
- Aged 45-65
- Married, with three children
- Lives in Boca Raton, Florida
- Household income $100K+

Psychographics (informed by the Internet):

- Health and diet conscious
- Busy lifestyle (based on LinkedIn work profile and school website logins)
- Purchases groceries at one specific market (based on loyalty card data)
- Surfs the internet in the evenings for pleasure
- Prefers Pinterest as a social network
- Buys monthly from Etsy and Amazon
- Purchases quality
- Always uses two-day shipping
- Reads articles mostly about recipes, psychology/self-help and health/nutrition

If you combine both of the data sets, you get a pretty clear vision about what this woman might like to purchase in the future. That information allows advertisers to purchase advertising targeted at this specific profile of person. The advertisers and their agencies can also cross these data points with other similar profiles to come up with new ideas about what a similar type of woman might like to buy. If, for example, 90% of women with similar profiles took an online course in Yoga, that advertiser might want to purchase a Facebook ad with this new persona or demographic/psychographic profile as the target.

The Supposition Headline

As we discussed earlier, headlines are important for reasons both psychological (persuasion) and technical (SEO). When it comes to news headlines, there are some variations that you should be aware of. One of these we'll call the "supposition headline." Here's how it works. It's best to use a specific example. Take a look at this headline:

WHITE HOUSE

Trump's tariff war nudges Cohn toward White House exit

The president's top economic adviser lost a battle to prevent the imposition of steep tariffs pushed by protectionist advisers.

By BEN WHITE and ANDREW RESTUCCIA | 03/01/2018 04:50 PM EST | Updated 03/01/2018 08:01 PM EST

Gary Cohn, President Donald Trump's top economic adviser, nearly quit last summer following the president's comments about a white supremacist march in Charlottesville, Virginia. | Alex Wong/Getty Images

Gary Cohn, President Donald Trump's top economic adviser, has been rumored to be on the brink of leaving the White House for months but stayed for one main reason: to stop the president from imposing steep tariffs.

By Thursday afternoon, Cohn had lost the fight.

MOST READ

It starts with a very subject verb: "nudges."

If this were a hard news story, the word nudges wouldn't be used, so you can assume from the get-go that this is a news analysis piece even though it may be masquerading as hard news. What's being supposed here is simple – Cohn might leave the white house team because of the trade war. It turns out Cohn did resign days after this story, so the journalist who produced it was onto something. However, there were no known facts about the supposition at the time of this article's publication. Would Cohn get fired? Would he resign? Would he be demoted? It wasn't known at the time. So, this was speculative news . . . and not really news as such. Let's examine the text of the article to gain a little more clarity on this speculation. We've highlighted the salient issues:

> Gary Cohn, President Donald Trump's top economic adviser, has been rumored to be on the brink of leaving the White House for months but stayed for one main reason: to stop the president from imposing steep tariffs.

. . .

> The decision came after a frantic 24 hours in which Cohn and others tried to talk Trump off the ledge. At one point, aides were sure Trump would make the announcement. Then they said he wouldn't. Finally, sitting alongside steel executives, he did.

> The Dow promptly tanked over 500 points, and Cohn's allies began wondering if this would be the final insult sending the director of the National Economic Council to the exit.

> One person close to Cohn, a former Goldman Sachs executive, said he wouldn't be surprised if he eventually left the chaotic and deeply exhausting administration as a result of the decision. A second person close to Cohn described it as a brutal blow that violated one of the NEC director's core beliefs—that protectionism is economically backward and won't lead to increased prosperity.

First, the "has been rumored" bit does not name a source. Right away, we can dispense with this article and understand that it's purely speculative. If we want facts, we're done. If we want supposition, we can continue reading. In the past, journalists were required to provide sources for their claims. These days it's not so common.

". . . others tried to talk Trump off the ledge." This is more supposition. As if the journalist were in the room when a particular meeting took place, the story adds some drama and a big metaphor to spice things up. This frames the trade issue as one that's *suicidal!* There's a whole lot of subjective guessing going on there. The word "frantic" also adds to the drama.

Next, the Dow drops 500 points. By linking the hypothetical suicidal meeting with economic events, the article claims some causality. No one really knows why the market drops. That's a guess plain and simple. Maybe it's true, maybe it's not. But to claim it as fact is just that . . . a claim.

The last paragraph continues the drama and supposition. There's another unnamed source (from a company with thousands of employees). Who knows who it was? "Chaotic" and "exhausting" are subjective assumptions. How does this source know? Were they in the meeting? Someone else unnamed characterizes it as "brutal" – more drama and license taken by the journalist. Finally, we get a sweeping generalization about protectionism that's neither proven nor agreed upon. However, it's presented as absolute fact. The article projects this belief onto the National Economic Council (NEC) chairman without asking the chairman himself. There is no attribution.

The ability to spot these kinds of articles and break them down, noticing the subjectivity involved and the appearance of drama, is an important skill. If you can do this consistently, you can maintain a clearer idea about what's actually hard news and what's pure speculation. You'll notice that much of speculative news is aligned with specific ideological goals. In this case, it's about the negative consequences of protectionism, and there's some flavor in there that wants the reader to absorb just how chaotic, crazy and brutal the white house affairs have become. We don't know if any of that is true, but the article makes a great case for it. That's the beauty (and the trap) of supposition and engaging, lively, emotional writing.

How to Filter News Stories for "Fake News" Attributes – 9 Strategies

1. *Look up the author of the article.* You can examine other articles they've written and even Wikipedia them to see more about their life backgrounds, political leanings, past works and future endeavors.

2. *Make a judgement about the publisher.* There is quite a bit of information out in the world about publications, their political alignment and their purpose/mission. Some will tell you straight up. Others don't advertise this. It's up to you to compare and contrast stories across different publications and either confirm your own biases or challenge your beliefs. It can be fun – or maddening! This tool is useful for gauging factual reporting levels and pinpointing left/right/center political alignment. https://mediabiasfactcheck.com

3. *Consider the sources quoted (or not quoted) in the story.* It's very common these days to use un-attributed sources with lines like the following: "these people said," "according to people familiar with the matter," and "scientists said." This is a new development and was not previously allowed in serious news rooms. Nowadays everyone does it. You could call it The National Enquirer-ization of media. If you see this, you can bet the article's or broadcast's producers do not have all the information yet, or they don't have credible sources. They're just trying to scoop the story and get ahead of competitive media outlets. Sites like TMZ and Buzzfeed engage in the practice consistently.

4. *Verify*. If you must believe something, try to verify it across a wide range of outlets, like other media publications, Wikipedia, Snopes and a handful of reputable national and international newspapers. Reputable is the operative word here. It's subjective, I know. Put it through your schooling filter, too. Do the math. Question the numbers. See if it's contrary to physics and known scientific principles.

5. *Verify via Google reverse image search*. Here's the URL: https://reverse.photos/ . Sometimes lazy journalists and scammers with an axe to grind will use old, proven-powerful images to bolster their current article. You can save the photo and see if it was used previously and in social media posts at an earlier time. If you find it elsewhere, then the article is probably bogus in some way. Journalist and TV personality Katie Couric fell for this during 2017's hurricane Harvey. She posted this photo from her friend on Twitter:

The problem is that the photo was from months earlier. This type of photo re-use has been common in Middle East conflicts, where photos of dead children and innocent people are repurposed to stoke public outrage.

6. *Consider the information's origins.* Fake URLs that are close in spelling to the real news site's are common. Here's a funny one that actually redirects to a site about Fake News (looks like some

guy's portfolio of the fake news he's produced successfully!): denverguardian.com

7. Read a few articles on the site and make up your own mind about whether the information is accurate, salacious, misleading, etc. This is self-explanatory. It can be a little daunting or confusing, however. Some publications famously broke major news stories, while a lot of the other content on their pages was of dubious factual foundation. This is the curious case of the National Enquirer and O.J. Simpson. Somehow that widely panned publication got leaks about the case, or they were doing actual hard-nosed reporting, and they broke a lot of the most true and factual stories about that famous murder case. Look it up!

8. Put headlines through a neutral/not neutral filter. Take a look at a few news headlines, and you'll quickly get the hang of this. What you're looking for are indications of fact (neutral who, what, where, when words in the headline) and subjective spin (why and how words that assume specific positions or ideological slants).

Here's an example of a neutral headline:

Recreational Pot Is Officially Legal in California

By **THOMAS FULLER** JAN. 1, 2018

It's a recitation of a current events fact. It's got the what and the where. There's no attempt to explain how or why, or give it any other kind of editorial spin.

Here's one that's got a lot of "opinion" and "angle" in the headline (it's from someone's Twitter feed):

There's some who, plus some opinion (How do they know he's colluding? By the photo?), and some judgement about who the people are, as in 'elites.' The rest doesn't make much sense, because there's probably a typo by omission here (the word 'to').

> *9. Check your emotions: Are you angry, sad, provoked or triggered in some way.* This is a red flag. Your logical brain is short circuited when you're emotions react strongly to a story. This is a tough one, because part of the reason we read the news is to feel some sort of empathy. Hurricane victims, for example, elicit our sympathies. Some articles, however, are designed to provoke emotion, and they're not always trustworthy in this regard.

Here are some crazy, emotionally provocative headlines from the "paid advertising" portion of BuzzFeed.com's site:

This Photographer Captured His
Brother Choking On McDonald's
And The Photos Are Hilarious

23 Pictures People Who Went To
Private School Will Never
Understand

Build The Ultimate Kids Meal And
We'll Guess Your Real Age And
Emotional Age

This one's just weird, and might just piss off some people (it originated from the site Vice.com):

► 2:18

Is Watching Harry Potter Porn Weird?

On this episode of 'Ask SLUTEVER,' VICE's resident sexpert Karley Sciortino weighs in on fantasizing about witches and wizards.

These headlines provoke a wide array of emotions and feelings. The choking headline stirs up concern, then some prospect of humor, then a bit of lingering disturbance as you wonder what could possibly be funny about a brother choking in a restaurant. The second one evokes disgust and curiosity while playing into a class issue regarding public vs. private schools (common people vs. elites). The third headline links to a quiz that directly promises information about the quiz-taker's emotional state. The final one from Vice.com hints at extreme perversion and all the curiosity and disgust that might entail. The idea that they have a staff "sexpert" is kind of ridiculous. This is certainly click bait that is, in a really off-putting and icky way, aimed at kids and the older generation that grew up on Harry Potter books. It's hijacking the Harry Potter platform in some sense. Like "newsjacking," it takes a highly popular theme – the J.K. Rowling books – and piggy backs on their wide keyword and societal appeal. It's pretty lame.

Updated Note About BuzzFeed

Up to this point, we've bashed on BuzzFeed a fair amount. Historically, the site played punching bag to media snobs who prefer the *New York Times* and the *Washington Post* to lesser news outlets.

Things have changed, however. The International Symposium on Online Journalism showed some new data demonstrating the BuzzFeed now acts a bit more like a traditional news operation.

> ". . . BuzzFeed has gradually adopted routines resulting in more hard news stories, thus beginning to appear like other more "mature" news organizations. . . BuzzFeed is featuring more sources, more hard news."

Interestingly, BuzzFeed, which is a digital-only news source, reported a net profit of $2.7 million for the first half of 2014. That's a significant number for a news organization. Most newspapers across the country report significant losses, and many are flirting with bankruptcy. That profitability wasn't unnoticed. NBCUniversal invested $200 million in BuzzFeed in 2015. That's also a bit staggering and certainly notable, because now BuzzFeed has to answer to the powers that be at NBC. And, as we'll discover moving forward, NBC isn't the most pristine of news outlets when it comes to knuckling under to political pressure and running news that's clearly native advertising. All these publications and digital outlets succumb to the same advertising pressure the big networks caved into over the decades.

Here's the link to the full report from ISOJ: http://bit.ly/2r9reIf

The report details a BuzzFeed interview with President Obama in 2015 titled "BuzzFeed Presents: Things Everybody Does But Doesn't Talk About." The video, in which Obama mugs on camera and eventually promotes a deadline to sign up for Obamacare, got more than 22 million views on YouTube. As noted in the report, this is the kind of integrated digital media that reaches millennials, an audience coveted by old-guard media like NBC. The report noted: ". . it is hard to imagine a similar video could have been produced by a legacy media company such as *The Wall Street Journal* or *The New York Times*." Truth is, BuzzFeed is now becoming very similar to those traditional outlets. They just use snazzier headlines and have serious clickbait skills on their editorial staff.

Warnings About the News "Industry"

Unlike a lot of other industries that have clear motivations about what's being sold and purchased, the combined news/advertising industry is problematic. The fact that most publications rely on advertising to support their business introduces complicating factors. They need money to support their operations, and they'll get very creative in that pursuit. The problem shows up with political reporting, too.

To explain, let's look at some revealing outtakes from *Persuasion in Society* by Herbert Simons and Jean Jones:

> ". . . former *Washington Post* reporter Mike Allen (July 3, 2009) brought news to *Politico* that the Post was offering lobbyists "off-the-record dinner and discussion" with top congressional and administration officials for $25,000 a plate, first on the topic of health care."

Tim Graham, an online columnist who was critical of that invitation to lure in lobbyists and money complication said:

"the offer – which essentially turns a news organization into a facilitator for private lobbyist-official encounters – is a new sign of the lengths to which news organizations will go to find revenue at a time when most newspapers are struggling for survival."

The general problem here is that the "front office" in an industry that's facing immense pressures with respect to economic viability has been increasingly placing demands on their news gathering organizations. They need to see profits to keep the publications in business. Many a news room has been urged to "think corporate" as they develop their stories. That's a serious problem if your publication is involved in any sort of truth telling. More from *Persuasion in Society*:

> "executives agreed to run a special issue of the *Los Angeles Times* Sunday magazine devoted exclusively to favorable coverage of a new downtown sports arena. Contractors and patrons were strongly encouraged to advertise. Not disclosed in the news coverage was that the *Times* was a secret partner in the arena project and that it was to share in the profits from the magazine advertising."

Here's the kicker that defines the issue at hand. The book quotes Max Frankel, a distinguished journalist for the *New York Times*:

> "A wall is needed to insulate the gathering of news, which should be a selfless public service, from the pursuit of profit, which is needed to guarantee the independence of the business. *Journalism, in other words, is a costly and paradoxical enterprise*: It can flourish only when profitable, but it is most suspect when it seeks a profit at all costs. (Frankel, 2000) (my

emphasis is in italics)

We're going to talk about movie product placement later in this book, but it's worth bringing up here in the context of these book excerpts. *Persuasion in Society* goes on to say:

> "If ever there was a wall between entertainment programming and product advertising, it has long since been broken with the advent of MTV, of kids' shows specifically designed to promote featured products, and of product displays surreptitiously inserted into feature films. But these deceptions are relatively benign when measured against news that the government has also been attempting to persuade in the guise of entertainment (Romano, 200). A few years ago, the White House negotiated a deal with the television networks, forgiving them an obligation to provide so many minutes of unpaid public service advertising in return for their agreement to insert the government's pro-social messages into prime-time dramas such as *Touched by an Angel, NYPD Blue, ER, Beverly Hills 90210,* and *Chicago Hope.*

We're going to cover public service deals in popular entertainment further in Part 6 of this book and in our section on *transactional journalism in* Part 3. Stay tuned. For now, let's finish out the story with this particular White House dilemma. The book continued:

> "Arguably this was a good deal for the networks. Their estimated gain would be approximately $22 million worth of added time for paid advertising. The cost would be a small reduction in their once vaunted reputation for creative independence. Television writers would not be forced to change their scripts, and the government would not be asking television producers to promote its more controversial activities – only to insert into their prime-time scripts subtle messages about the dangers of street

drugs and alcohol. Somehow, though, the ethics of this deal seem questionable.

The book notes Georgetown University law professor David Cole's take on the issue:

> ". . . the government is not supposed to favor the content of one message over another when doling out financial benefits to facilitate private speech. They crossed the line between government speech and private speech, and basically coerced private speakers, through the public purse, into expressing government messages in a way that was designed to mislead the American public. The rights the U.S. government violated in this case were the rights of viewers and listeners not to be propagandized in an underhanded way by their leaders (Romano, 2000).

This is just another form of *Media Collusion*.

Part 3 – News "Experts"

"When you are unconscious, you are being thought by the collective mind."

– Eckhart Tolle

The public is fed news stories by all kinds of different personalities and journalists. Some of them are very skilled at their trade and have specific expertise in subject matter. Unfortunately, a lot of them are not experts in anything other than looking good on camera, articulating sentences that are fed to them via teleprompters, and asking questions that seem to be relevant. These questions, by the way, are often fed to the "on air talent" through an earpiece via producers who are smarter than the talent and have more expertise in the particular topic.

There are also writers/journalists who are not particularly expert at any one thing but have great skill in describing things and interviewing experts. I'm reminded of a shoe that Nike once sold back in the 1990s called the Nike Cross-Trainer. It was kind of a head scratcher. The shoe was not good for any particular sport or exercise but kind of okay for a wide range of activities. Not great for anything in particular . . . decent for all kinds of things. Stupid, right? Well, the modern world of reporting and publishing is filled with these kinds of people. They're good communicators, but they have no apparent skill in vetting facts or putting an expert lens on a particular topic or event. This results in inaccuracies, misreporting and general miscommunication.

These kinds of shortcomings can be particularly obvious with broadcast news anchors (the more local and small town they get the lower the quality, usually). To be fair, as a print journalist, I've got some prejudices against the "on air talent." News anchors have a unique skill set that requires an ability to read news from a teleprompter while hearing other instructions through a speaker in their ear. They're good at, perhaps to the detriment of other skills. They're not known across the industry to be good researchers, writers or otherwise competent thinkers. If you delve into the backgrounds, education and training of these people, you'll see that they typically come from broadcast journalism programs at communications schools and are almost always backed up by academics from Ivy League schools in the control booths and at the writing tables. They're essentially puppets, and they're reading news in every community across the country.

Not a lot of journalists have specific industry or topical expertise. If you have any relatives or friends that are pilots or doctors or NASA scientists, for example, you're probably familiar with the mistakes reporters make. My dad was a pilot (USAF and professional jet pilot), and I always pick his brain when an airplane tragedy hits the news. He immediately uncovers all the BS and blatant mistakes that the journalists make when they're reporting the story. This stuff just happens because of the nature of the journalism beast. Pilots aren't writing for the L.A. Times

– they're flying airplanes. The number and frequency of the mistakes in the articles are appalling, however. "Facts" can quickly become skewed and misunderstood via this expert disconnect process. News organizations try to get around this by putting experts on camera and microphone, and in quotes in written articles. Even then, on air talent will misconstrue sound bites, editorially manipulate the message, and generally botch the information. Misquoting is rampant in print publications, as well. If you've ever been misquoted by a journalist, you know this to be true.

So it's important to consider the roles of those who create the news. There are generally three different types of "on air" talent (other than news readers/anchors) and "between the pages" talent.

#1: The Reporter: A reporter is supposed to give dry, unadulterated information back - what's often termed "hard news" - to the news publisher, whether that's a broadcast news outfit, an editorial room or a website publishing team. The reporter is perhaps the most legitimate cog in the machine of the news organization, because they're tasked with bringing in facts and offering them up without editorial or analytical filters. These days, however, the reporter has been compromised. Most reporters offer up an editorial-style filter on their opinion. They bake in opinion or Op-Ed flavor to their reports. This is something that's human, so it's very subtle. In the past, reporters were only allowed to deliver Who, What, Where, When and How information about their specific assignments. Today, however, you get all kinds of smug input that has been designed to bring in more casual viewership and develop the Why. Somewhere along the line, news organizations decided it was important to bring in viewers via tone and style. It's probably an affectation or carry over from the daytime television shows like Donahue, Ellen, The View or whatever show that appeared to connect with people that were ill-informed but just wanted to connect popular issues back to their lives.

#2 The Journalist: A journalist has a different role or is a more generalized definition than that of reporter. Reporters are journalists, and journalists certainly report the news. Traditionally, however, a journalist wrote a personal account of an event, situation or development. A reporter, on one hand, is dealing with facts about developments. A journalist, however, puts a story over the facts. Journalists are in the tradition of Joan Didion or Hunter Thompson. They view reporter events and put a personal filter over the events. It's not necessarily going as far as news analysis (see below). Truman Capote's *In Cold Blood* is a good example of this type of writing and reporting. It's very matter of fact and tries to steer clear of making judgements, but it's definitely the writer's or producer's story to present. Their input adds a flavor and narrative to the events being reported. This can be long form, as in Truman Capote's book, or short form in the pages of a newspaper or blog. That said, the lines between reporter, journalist and news analyst are quite blurry these days.

#3 The News Analyst: News analysis was traditionally a job reserved for broadcasters and Opinion/Editorial writers who put a critical eye on news stories. They allow their own subjective opinions and research to color their take on a particular event or development. Nowadays, everyone's a news analyst, it seems. The popular broadcast shows on cable TV, like CNN, MSNBC and Fox News have a majority of their programming filled with shows that try to analyze and put political and social spins on the events of the day. These programs intersperse "hard reporting" between breaks and often have the on-air personality report breaking news as it happens. For the sake of generality, I'd place opinion/editorial (OpEd) writers and producers into this grouping.

That's a high level view of the three major news production buckets. There is, however, a bonus category that's somewhat new, that we'll call **Celebrity Journalist**. This takes several forms and is probably an evolution of the nightly news anchor (people like Walter Cronkite and Edward R. Murrow). It doesn't necessarily have to be a news anchor, however. Some examples:

- Bill O'Reilly
- Rachel Maddow
- Chris Matthews
- Katie Couric
- Bill Nye the Science Guy

- Bryant Gumbel
- Charlie Rose
- Matt Lauer
- Dan Rather
- Mike Wallace
- Megyn Kelly
- Joy Behar

The list is pretty long. Those are just a few. This category of news presenter/analyst builds a special bond with their audience. They're often beloved by their followers and have a significant amount of sway over the opinions, orientations and attitudes of their audiences. On the other hand, they often are put off by or despised by others who do not share their same political opinions and interpretations of events. They tend to take stands and positions that follow very established or entrenched political lines. In the current social media climate, they tend to get a lot of attention and stir up controversy outside of regular working hours because they have significant numbers of followers and can influence lots of people all at once with respect to certain issues or events.

There are all kinds of other workers that contribute to the making and dispersion of news. Here's a short list of some of the more salient players:

- **Broadcast editors** – These people edit news stories that funnel in from reporters and journalists. They shape the news by putting their personal filters onto the topics, omitting or including certain facts, and "tightening" up the stories. We talked about this editing earlier when we discussed how news isn't really ever objective, even when it's a "hard news" story on the front page of a newspaper or web site. Humans select the news, so their agendas and proclivities tend to creep in. Broadcast editors will often examine print press releases, video press releases and audio press releases to consider what kinds of things to include in their broadcasts.

- **Print editors** – These editors play a role similar to the broadcast editor, except in print. They'll often pore through print press releases to select which stories to run in their publications.
- **Program directors** – This is similar to the broadcast editor and the names are synonymous. They select content that goes into their broadcasts. Some program directors actually manage show segments as they're developing, as well. They're like movie directors that are working on the fly as new information comes in.
- **Publishers** – This could be anyone from a blogger to a book publisher. When you hear the word "content," that's what they're putting out into the world. But content can mean any type of media, from a documentary movie to an infographic. It's very general these days. In the past, a publisher was a journal, almanac, book, reference resource, or other print-based creator. This moved into CD-ROM and software publishing, then blog, web site, YouTuber, podcaster, etc.
- **Producers** (TV vs. Hollywood/Movies) – The movie/TV dichotomy is quite large. Hollywood movie producers wear many hats, but they're primarily involved in raising money for the film, guiding it creatively, and choosing the right people to work on it (director, actors, production designers and other creatives). TV producers are more like program directors. In a live newscast, they sit in a broadcast booth and direct the show via a microphone that goes into the ears of the camera people and on air talent. TV producers that create television entertainment shows are more like their movie business counterparts.
- **Bloggers and Alt-Media** – There are all kinds of bloggers out there, from foodie bloggers to financial experts, but we're talking about news bloggers here. Some are just story aggregators – like The Drudge Report and The Huffington Post (although the HuffPo has its own writers). Aggregators like The Drudge Report craft an editorial theme (conservative and provocative like tabloids) then only share links that fit that theme. Others are very wild and

outrageous prognosticators that have very specific agendas to push. Think Milo Yiannopoulos, Michelle Malkin, Daily Kos, TownHall, and The Nation.

Snopes: What Is It, and Can You Trust It?

Snopes is a site that's been confirming and debunking all kinds of online and offline legends, facts, stories and hoaxes for quite some time.

Who's behind it? It was started by a husband and wife team in 1996 and evolved into its current form by depending on Google AdWords ads for revenue. In 2017 the site raised $700,000 via a GoFundMe.com campaign.

The site has made and corrected errors over the years. It's an evolving encyclopedia of fact and fiction review that's useful for researching questionable claims that you come across online.

The husband now heads up the site and the wife no longer works there. He has said that the site generates more complaints of liberal bias than conservative.

There have always been unconfirmed rumors that billionaire activist George Soros funds the site.

If you think Snopes is biased on a particular issue or fact, you can use standard Google searches to further vet facts about myths or suspected hoaxes.

How to Evaluate News Pros that Want to Grab Your Attention

If you want to figure out who's an expert and who knows what they're talking about, the web is your friend. A Wikipedia search on any relevant writer, reporter or broadcast news journalist will turn up all kinds of relevant information about their education, work background, biases, books written, content produced and so forth.

You should make it a practice to vet journalists and broadcasters in order to figure out if how much influence you let them have over your opinions. This is particularly useful when examining the backgrounds of news analysts and bloggers. TV news organizations draw heavily on government bureaucrats and former intelligence agency workers (hint: spies) to put analytical filters onto the events of the day. If you're watching the news with a laptop or tablet nearby, you can quickly learn a lot more about these people, the organizations they're affiliated with, and their past positions. With just a little reading, you can get to know who they really are and why they may have come into favor with the particular news production. The people who appear on Fox, for example, are often very different than those that appear on CNN. The two channels are politically polarized. There are some that regularly appear on both channels. It's worth looking into all of them if you want to have a really objective view into why they say what they do.

If you want to vet specific stories, again the internet is your friend. You'll come across all manner of conflicting debate in alternate stories, comment threads and various other screeds. Some will be useful, but some will be complete and total nonsense. This is where the difficult part of vetting stories comes in. You have to rely on your own common sense views of the world and how it works to make decisions about what's accurate and what's not.

One of the more common story vetting tactics employed by professional journalists is called "follow the money." When you consider issues within a context that places strong significance on the observation that humans invariably are motivated and take action in line with economic incentives, you can uncover some very valuable insights. This isn't always the case, of course. People are motivated by altruism, justice, racism, gender bias, worldview bias, hunger, fear, irrationality and much more, but as time goes on and people get older, money can become a very accurate predictor of behavior. We'll talk more about "follow the money" in Part 6.

Exercise: Pick two TV news personalities – anchor, reporter or analyst/opinion contributor – and read through their Wikipedia entries. If you find anything that surprises you or interests you about their backgrounds, take down some notes and share it with us when we reconvene.

How to Spot Political Talking Points?

As you consume news media, you'll eventually come across something that analysts and news people of every stripe call "talking points." What are these things, and how can you spot them?

This is pretty fun. In the U.S., the two major political parties often respond to issues and events with pre-planned responses that are designed for media consumption. What you need to realize (a fact which most media consumers don't fully consider) is that each party, as well as each of the major branches of government and government departmental groups (think Homeland Security, CIA, Department of Defense and so on), employs large public relations organizations and teams of speechwriters and issue response analysts that are ready to craft messaging for any type of potential news event. The messages they craft are called talking points, and they're created on the fly as news develops.

Let's say, for example, that a shooting takes place at a school or on a subway in a major city. Typical Democratic party talking points will place an analysis filter over the event which adds the need for gun control laws to be expanded within the country. The typical Republican talking points will call for more law enforcement measures and increased spending on police and security resources. It's not always this way, but these are the common themes.

The cool thing is that there's a way to use the internet to see if the article you're reading or the broadcast you just watched is using these talking points. All you have to do is copy and paste a phrase that seems like a talking point from an article. Put quotes around that phrase, and then search Google for the phrase.

People compile these on YouTube. Here's a political talking points clip:

Media Demands 'No Matter Your Politics' You Respect Clinton's Historic Achievement | SUPERcuts! #330

9,958 views

http://bit.ly/2qZkCfu

The talking point is "no matter what your politics, this is an historic moment." The reference is to Hillary Clinton's nomination as a presidential candidate. Some of the anchors try to vary the talking point, and a few mess it up because they're not very good at getting creative on their feet. For the most part, however, they deliver the line straight from the teleprompter as it's written.

Here's another humorous compilation of this phenomenon in action:

Mindless Media: News anchors from over a dozen US networks all reading the same script.

http://bit.ly/2r3w7ma

The anchors all use the same phrase – "economic factors may take some of the spring out of the Easter Bunny's step this year" – then go on to cover whatever economic news relates to the declaration. It's repeated dozens of times in the YouTube clip. This is a dead giveaway that the newscast is running the story verbatim and it was crafted by some other outfit or organization (usually a PR company, a government agency or a non-profit organization). Interestingly, none of the anchors decided they'd customize the script for their own broadcast. Why get creative when you can just read a prompter?

You can find talking points via Google fairly easily for print articles, as well. First, what you do is identify a story that's bound to generate conflicting responses from both political parties. What are some good topics or events?

- Public shootings
- Terrorist attacks
- Gun-based murders
- Economic calamities (like stock market crashes – mini and big)
- Worker strikes
- Election controversies (like ballot recounts during close elections)
- Violent crimes by migrants
- Violent protests at universities

Find an article on that particular event that's headlining one of the major news outlets like ABC, CBS, CNN, FOX, NBC, or PBS. Next, you want to read through the article and look for quotes from politicians or spokespeople that have some hint of or blatant bias baked in. For example, you might find a Democratic congressional spokesperson that's interviewed saying that gun laws need to be toughened up after a high-profile shooting takes place.

Here's an organization that publishes specific talking points and how to strategize after a shooting event:

Gun Messaging

Voicing Our Values—To Curtail Gun Violence

This is an addendum to our book, *Voicing Our Values: A Message Guide for Candidates.* Our purpose is to help lawmakers, candidates and activists understand how to argue in favor of current proposals to curtail gun violence. As we explain here, we have tried to make this resource as easy-to-use as possible by placing model language in boxes throughout. We encourage you to adapt the language to your own voice and personalize it with your own knowledge and experience. Much more comprehensive, detailed or technical talking points are available from advocacy groups listed at the end of this paper.

QUICK LINKS:

- How to introduce your argument
- About Background Checks
- About Military-Style Assault Weapons
- About High-Capacity Ammunition Magazines
- How to rebut common pro-gun arguments
- Sources for more detailed talking points
- **A PDF copy of** Voicing Our Values—To Curtail Gun Violence

Our most important advice: (1) Lay out the problem in very simple terms—most Americans have no idea how easy our laws make it for dangerous people to buy handguns and assault weapons; (2) Don't let pro-gun advocates sidetrack the debate into "straw man" arguments, obscure "facts," or a focus on the technical properties of guns—about 90 percent of their arguments are actually designed to change the subject so you need to insist on a debate that is relevant to the legislation at hand; and (3) Generally:

Download the Book

Buy it on Amazon

http://bit.ly/2qZtHop

GUN MESSAGING
PROGRESSIVE
MAJORITY ACTION

So, what happens when we clip one of the phrases from that page and put it into a Google search? I took the phrase "keep guns out of the hands of dangerous people" from that site and popped it into Google within quotes. Here's the result:

All   Shopping   News   Images   Videos   More   Settings   Tools

About 22,600 results (0.70 seconds)

Petition · Keep Guns Out of the Hands of Dangerous People · Change ...
https://www.change.org/p/keep-guns-out-of-the-hands-of-dangerous-people ▾
Every day, 34 Americans are murdered with guns, and we can't accept the flaws in our background check system that lead to these tragic deaths. The recent shooting in Tucson is another tragic reminder of how easy it is for dangerous people to get their hands on guns. Our gun laws are designed to prevent felons, the ...

Keep guns out of hands of dangerous people | Visit Us at the Kennett ...
https://gunsensecc.com/2016/09/18/keep-guns-out-of-hands-of-dangerous-people/ ▾
Sep 18, 2016 - Compare with Canada- 2.3 and Great Britain- less than 1 gun death per 100,000, and you can see that the best safety measure is not bullet proof glass, or active shooter drills. It is doing everything you can to **keep guns out of the hands of dangerous people**. Tom Buglio Chester County Coalition to Prevent ...

Keeping guns Out Of The Hands Of Dangerous People Reduces ...
https://law.stanford.edu/press/keeping-guns-hands-dangerous-people-reduces-violence/ ▾
Jul 7, 2017 - He's wrong; common-sense laws **keep guns out of the hands of dangerous people** and reduce gun violence. There are numerous studies that prove the point. The "guns everywhere" outlook of Mr. Ambrose defies logic. As Shannon Watts, founder of Moms Demand Action, said, "If loose gun laws and more ...

An Open Letter To Amazon About Gun Violence Prevention
https://www.bradycampaign.org/an-open-letter-to-amazon-about-gun-violence-preve... ▾
At the Brady Campaign and Center to Prevent Gun Violence, we support common-sense gun laws that **keep guns out of the hands of dangerous people**, making our nation safer. We know that you want Amazon employees to be safe from gun violence. Brady urges you to consider the strength of local and state gun laws ...

Keep Guns Out Of Dangerous Hands In Orlando, In Chicago, In Every ...
https://www.huffingtonpost.com/.../keep-guns-out-of-dangerous-hands_b_10532466... ▾
Jun 18, 2016 - That's why we are pushing in Washington to **keep guns out of the hands of dangerous people**. There are simple steps Congress can and must take to end this gun violence nightmare: We must make universal background checks the law of the land, and close a shocking loophole in current law that allows ...

Is Gun Violence Due To Dangerous People Or Dangerous Guns? - NPR
https://www.npr.org/...7/.../is-gun-violence-due-to-dangerous-people-or-dangerous-guns ▾
Aug 31, 2015 - ... emphasizing either dangerous people or dangerous guns. For instance, the news story emphasizing dangerous people included the following: " With more than 65,000 Americans shot in an attack last year, we have to do something to **keep guns out of the hands of dangerous people**, said Kim Jones, ...

Let's see. Major news outlets like the Huffington Post and NPR used the phrase in their posts verbatim, and 22,600 results came up in the Google search. That's a talking point. You can do this whenever you hear or see a phrase that seems like it's a talking point. This happens a lot on broadcast news channels. If you were to watch several local and national newscasts' treatments of the same hot political topic, for example, you'll often find that all of them use the same phrasing taken from party talking points and/or major news publications like the Washington Post or the New York Times. Local and national broadcasts recognize that you're not a news analyst, and they won't try to hide the fact that they're using the same phrasing. The typical news consumer isn't going to read three newspapers and watch several news broadcasts on TV, so they can get away with using the same phrase. It's part laziness and part towing the party lines.

Here's another example of organization-driven talking points from the conservative press about mental disorders and gun laws. I found the phrase in this article about fact checking conservative claims: http://bit.ly/2r1pH6Z

EDITIONS ⌄ TRUTH-O-METER™ ⌄ PEOPLE ⌄ PROMISES ⌄ PANTS ON FIRE ABOUT US ⌄

Fact-checking the NRA's response to proposed gun laws after Las Vegas

By Jon Greenberg on Tuesday, October 10th, 2017 at 5:13 p.m.

The National Rifle Association called for a review of regulations on the sales of the "bump stock" devices. The devices were used by the Las Vegas gunman to rapidly fire semi-automatic rifles like machine guns Oct. 1.

This is the important phrase: "help handling their finances." I highlighted it from the context of the article in this clip about Chris Cox:

> **"Cox: The Social Security Administration's "definition of a mental disorder was someone who asked for help handling their finances. That is not a prohibitive category, Chris, and it shouldn't be a prohibitive category."**
>
> "Cox made it sound as though all it would take is someone asking for help with their personal finances to get swept up by a Social Security policy of sharing names for background check purposes. The process is more complicated."

If I take the phrase that's quoted in the interview and pump it into Google, I get a bunch of similar results in various other media outlets. That's a good indication that the talking point was common at the time.

Here's the Google result (next page):

the SSA rule ...

NRA's Chris Cox: Needing Help Handling Finances Shouldn't Prohibit ...
https://www.cnsnews.com/.../nras-chris-cox-needing-help-handling-finances-shouldnt... ▾
Oct 9, 2017 · Chris Cox, executive director of the National Rifle Association's Institute for Legislative
Action, on Sunday defended President Donald Trump's decision to overturn an Obama administration
directive requiring the Social Security Administration to submit the records of mentally disabled people
to the National ...

Steve Wynn on the future of security in Las Vegas - Android Lover
iandroidlove.com › worldwide News ▾
COX: Their **definition of a mental disorder was someone who asked for help handling their finances**.
That is not a prohibitive category, Chris, and it shouldn't be a prohibitive category. WALLACE: Let me ask
you about another measure that has been talked about, and before I do, I want you to just watch this
video. Here it is.

If you have a mental disability according to the SSA, you can get a ...
eqaultiyforall.blogspot.com/2017/11/if-you-have-mental-disability-according.html ▾
Cox: Their **definition of a mental disorder was someone who asked for help handling their finances**.
That is not a prohibitive category, Chris, and it shouldn't be a prohibitive category. [1]. Either Trump was
duped by the NRA into believing that this rule took away an elderly citizen's right to bear arms due to
their social security ...

Steve Wynn on the future of security in Las Vegas | Fox News
www.foxnews.com/transcript/2017/10/.../steve-wynn-on-future-security-in-las-vegas.ht...
Oct 8, 2017 · COX: Their **definition of a mental disorder was someone who asked for help handling their
finances**. That is not a prohibitive category, Chris, and it shouldn't be a prohibitive category. WALLACE:
Let me ask you about another measure that has been talked about, and before I do, I want you to just
watch this ...

As you can see, media outlets and their reporters tend to parrot each other. They take shortcuts in some cases, because deadlines are pressing, and it's easy to cut and paste. However, this practice is often related to political bias. A lot of media outlets that orient around polarizing conservative or liberal viewpoints take talking points to an extreme and use them far too frequently without questioning their origins or their veracity. This is how very significant positions or ideas are drilled into the public consciousness (dare I say the word brainwash?).

Why the "Wires" and the New York Times Are So Important

Way back when news was wired over telegraph to various newspapers around the country a few businesses started up. They were called "wire services," and they delivered news in wholesale fashion across the country and the world. One was called UPI for United Press International, another AP for Associated Press, and another Reuters (now Thomson Reuters), which was named after Paul Reuter. He developed his early business via homing pigeons and electric telephraphy. Interestingly, he started his business by distributing propaganda pamphlets about Europe's democratic reforms of 1848.

These news services all still exist in various forms, and they've consolidated somewhat across radio, print, TV and internet channels.

The larger point we want to develop here is about the origins of news stories. Traditionally, the AP, UPI, Reuters and several large national newspapers reported the lion's share of the news that was published across the

---

More on Paul Reuter from Wikipedia:

"A former bank clerk, in 1847 he became a partner in Reuter and Stargardt, a Berlin book-publishing firm. The distribution of radical pamphlets by the firm at the beginning of the 1848 [European] Revolution may have focused official scrutiny on Reuter.

"Later that year, he left for Paris and worked in Charles-Louis Havas' news agency, the future Agence France Presse.

"As telegraphy evolved, Reuter founded his own news agency in Aachen, transferring messages between Brussels and Aachen using carrier pigeons and thus linking Berlin and Paris. Speedier than the post train, pigeons gave Reuter faster access to financial news from the Paris stock exchange. Eventually, pigeons were replaced by a direct telegraph link.

U.S. Local newspapers certainly staffed their own reporters and journalists to cover local events, but a large portion of any given local newspaper's stories originated (or still originate) from only a few large pools of reportage, the most significant one being the New York Times.

The New York Times is a key component in the news scene, because a lot of the stories they run are repurposed elsewhere. Many of the phrases of NYT articles, for example, show up verbatim in local newscasts. Local newscasts are morning, mid-day and evening news show that run on conventional broadcast TV. KNBC Los Angeles is one example. They exist for every major city across the U.S., and they're still a significant source of news for Americans. Mother Jones reported in 2014 that 9 in 10 Americans view local news broadcasts, and 46% of those 9 watch it "often." So these newscasts are influential.

The problem is that as a media consumer, you only get one limited view of the world that's described by a group of reporters and writers at the NYT. This is not relegated to the Times. ABC, NBC, CBS, and Fox provide similar news content for their local affiliates, but even these outlets have an incestuous relationship with the Times. Stories from all of them end up within their pages and broadcasts. With the internet in play, there's even more overlap and duplication. One thing remains consistent, however. News comes from an increasingly aggregated set of publishers. Falling advertising prices and disruption in advertising models caused by the internet have put tremendous pressure on all kinds of publishing outlets, pushing them to consolidate and cut costs across all their operations. This presents the news consumer with less choice and fewer viewpoints and sources to read.

Here's an example of phrasing taken from a NYT article that made its way into a local newscast.

http://bit.ly/2r04Gtk

This example is another one of these duplicate stories similar to the Easter bunny story we covered earlier. The –

Here's some <u>follow-up analysis of that Conan goof</u>:

http://bit.ly/2r0zie3

CONAN COMEDY
BIT SERIOUS
ISSUES TV

You can read that at your leisure, but I want you to pay special attention to a particular passage, that's conveniently buried at the end of the article:

> "Some stations also edited key facts out of the story or presented it in ways that overhyped its premise. The original CNN report was largely based on a survey from the National Retail Federation, which annually asks people "if they plan to take advantage of sales or price discounts during the holiday season to make additional non-gift purchases." The survey concluded that self gifting has increased over the past decade, but consumers planned to slightly cut back on the practice this year.

> "KTNV in Las Vegas missed that subtlety when it called self gifting "a trend that's exploded." Meanwhile, KGUN in Tucson aired the story without attributing the data to the National Retail Federation or mentioning any source for the statistics at all. That's not a small omission, as retailers have a vested interest in promoting self gifting to help drive holiday sales."

Mother Jones also followed up on the trend: http://bit.ly/2HuOwDd

Here's the big nugget within that story:

> "In terms of dollar value, more than 75 percent of the nearly 300 full-power local TV stations purchased last year were acquired by just three media giants. The largest, Sinclair Broadcasting, will reach almost 40 percent of the population if its latest purchases are

approved by federal regulators. Sinclair's CEO has <u>said</u> he wants to keep snapping up stations until the company's market saturation hits 90 percent.

"Now here's where things *really* get sketchy: Media conglomerates such as Sinclair have bought up multiple news stations in the same regions—in nearly half of America's 210 television markets, one company owns or manages at least two local stations, and a lot of these stations now run very similar or even completely identical newscasts, according to a new report from the Pew Research Center. One in four local stations relies entirely on shared content."

They continue:

"And then there are stations like the CBS and NBC affiliates in Honolulu, which don't even bother staggering the times: They run identical newscasts simultaneously."

A news program simulcast by two Honolulu stations. **Pew Research Center**

And a final bit from the Mother Jones story:

"The stock value of Nexstar Broadcasting Group, which owns or services dual stations in 37 of its 56 markets, more than tripled last year. The value of Sinclair's stock more than doubled. Gannett's stock price jumped 34 percent the day that it announced that it was spending $2.2 billion to buy 17 TV news stations owned by Dallas-based Belo Corp. In addition to shaving operating costs, consolidation enables the increasingly powerful owners to negotiate much higher retransmission fees from cable providers."

So what's the takeaway here? News stories are not always original reporting. When you consume a news item in a vacuum – you're viewing what you think is an original instance, from a source that seems close to you and customized for your particular community or city – you're often consuming news that's been mass produced for the entire country. It just seems like it's local. This gets even more complicated when newscasts repurpose PR-generated content that's designed to make you behave in a certain way or purchase a specific product.

Native Advertising: News & Advertising Get Cozy

**"Advertising will only accelerate what
was going to happen anyway."**

– anonymous

There's responsibility and power that comes with business dominance. Let's take a look at how this works with one powerhouse brand: Starbucks. Contrary to what you might assume, Starbucks doesn't just serve up coffee.

Definition: Native Ad

na·tive ad·ver·tis·ing

noun

> material in an online publication which resembles the publication's editorial content but is paid for by an advertiser and intended to promote the advertiser's product.

"native advertising is blurring the lines between advertising and content"

This is from Google – the first search result, which Google somehow formats as its primary result. There is no attribution, as in Webster's Dictionary or Oxford Dictionary.

The definition is fairly limited, since native ads have been running in print publications for decades. David Ogilvy used them, and you can see them noted in magazines as "Advertising Supplement" or "Paid Promotion" or something similar. They're also all over the TV news, on cable and broadcast.

Yes, we know, they serve muffins, insanely sweet blended concoctions and weird cake-pops as well. But did you ever consider them a news publisher?

Probably not.

They are in the news game, though. Some of this is via their own outlets and blogs. Here are a couple of their publishing outlets:

https://1912pike.com and https://news.starbucks.com/

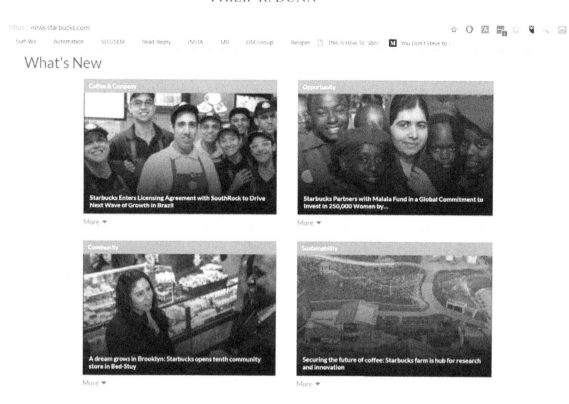

Somewhat less transparent is how Starbucks stories show up in the regular news media masquerading as real news.

In the following clip, you'll hear how ABC news treated two paying advertisers (Starbucks and Papa John's Pizza) and cashed in their advertising dollars during a national evening news broadcast.

http://bit.ly/2HtWc8S

Source credit: *No Agenda Show*

If you're reading the book on paper or on a device that doesn't follow links, head to this URL for the clip when you get a chance. It's fun. The following is the short summary for those reading text only. Read on to the next paragraph if you've heard the clip. *Summary:* A national news anchor reads teleprompter copy about how Starbucks is adding a new ingredient to their annual Pumpkin Spiced Latte. It now comes with real pumpkin! Hooray. That's the news. How fun. The next one is about how the founder of Papa John's pizza lost the car he originally sold to start the pizza chain. He sold it to finance the chain (according to lore), he bought it back, then it was mysteriously stolen and found right in time for this national news spot next to Starbucks.

The first bit about Starbucks is blatant. For years they've been trotting out the Pumpkin Spice Latte around the holidays. This particular year, they modified their story a little – "now with real pumpkin!" – in order to make it kind of a news story. What's ludicrous is that the nightly news would run such a story and treat it as if it's news. They'll talk all day long about "fake news" these days, but they're taking ad buys week in and week out to support these native ads. It's the same thing that BuzzFeed and Vox do, but it's supposed to be this pure, traditional, conventional media outlet that we all should trust to get our daily dose of what's real. It's not some web property with questionable backers. This is the national news that's been held up as a model of fairness and reliability for decades. These network news operations have been in business since the 1950's, guiding the American public about breaking events, wars, fires, weather disasters and the like.

The problem is that the modern format for TV news has been forced to change because of the internet and various other economic and viewer behavior changes. It used to be different. There was clear separation of advertising and news.

Take a look at these clips from 1960's broadcasts.

This one shows the intro to NBC news, and that the show it sponsored by Gulf Oil.

https://www.youtube.com/watch?v=EMPzDS-9rTI

http://bit.ly/2HspHIg

NBC NEWS
GULF OIL
SPECIAL REPORT

Here's the *summary for those of you without link access*: This clip is a 30-second intro to the news. It announces the news show and tells the viewer that it's sponsored by Gulf Oil, "producers of more and better energy from oil." Now that's separation.

Check the following clip at the 5-minute mark. You can skip through the initial five minutes of broadcast, unless you'd like to see how the sausage was made back in the 60's.

KGO News February 8 1965

http://bit.ly/2r0grzV

Notice that the anchor has a clear dividing line between the news and the advertisement. He says, "I'll be back with that story after this message." There's the news, and then there's the ad.

The line between advertising and news is quite clear. In the first clip, the show is sponsored an advertiser, and in the next one when they break for ads, there's clarity. The viewer has a distinct understanding of what is the news show and what is the advertising.

Today, however, the product buys into the show and displays itself as a news item. It's a little different with the Papa John's insertion, because it seems like there's a real story there. The car was stolen, but then it was recovered. If you have any background in PR, you'd be a bit more cynical. PR companies and the PR departments within large companies have been pulling stunts like this for years in order to gain media attention. If you combine a stunt that seems real with an ad buy that's either overt or "off the radar" (meaning, they want a story to run on the news hour – wink, wink – but they'll just buy future advertising and give the network a heads up when an intriguing story like a coveted car getting stolen happens).

The question you have to ask yourself is: How is it national news that the founder of Papa John's lost his car and found it a few days later? Was it headline news when the car was stolen? Did they follow up with a story the next day about how the thieves were captured and jailed? Did they follow up the next month when the thieves were sentenced? No. You get none of that, because the story is complete and utter hooey. It's an ad buy. Veiled or overt.

Here's one that's even more elegant and crafty. This is a native ad for Toys 'R Us. These run every year at Christmas time. Some years it's Toys 'R Us, some years it's Target, but it's always in play, because it's one of the more fool-proof scams around. The intro and outro for this clip includes some fun analysis from the a podcast that deconstructs news events. Part of their formula is to occasionally look at the advertising industry.

The news package was probably produced by Toys 'R Us, then distributed to local news stations. You can see this during Christmas when NBC affiliates, for example, run the same story with the same words in dozens of different markets across the country. The copy was crafted by the PR agency, not the news crews. Remember, they can get lazy and sometimes just use what they're given verbatim.

Click the clip here if you have access to links:

http://bit.ly/2roTexm Source credit: *No Agenda Show*

Here's the *summary*: The reporter talks about how a customer at Toys 'R Us put $200 on layaway to buy some Christmas items for her family. (Layaway, a system of paying a deposit to secure an item for later purchase, is a dated concept.) The story goes that some anonymous stranger paid off her layaway charges in the spirit of Christmas. At the end of the story, they claim that someone else in another state did the same thing to the tune of $20,000. Some random person paid off bills for $20k worth of toys. The piece even encourages people to get out there in case the trend continues! By the way, why not cover the $20,000 story and be done with it? That's way more than $200. My guess is that the local stations are pitched to use a local person and the local Toys 'R Us picks up the small expense so they can make the story local. The $20,000 bit at the end just sweetens the bit. It's so great!

So why have TV news networks been forced into this "native ad" game? Here's a short run down of the main factors in order of historical imperative (1926 – present day):

- Network competition – NBC (1926), CBS (1927) and ABC (1943)
- Local news competition (there are hundreds of NBC, CBS and ABC affiliates all across the nation) beating the nightly newscast to the punch on breaking stories
- VHF, UHF and 81 more channels (1950)
- Subscription TV - ON TV and SelecTV (1977)
- Cable TV and another 500 channels (Originated in 1948 but 1970-1980 is the era of HBO, Showtime, MTV, ESPN, CNN and the common channels we know today)
- CNN (1980)
- Discovery Channel, FX, NatGeo, etc.

- The internet (1992-1994 for the start of consumer adoption)
- Fox News (1996)
- Podcasts (2004)
- YouTube (2005)
- Cheap hand-held cameras (Flip camera- 2006)
- iPhone (2007)/mobile phone cameras/video
- Reality TV (1991 Holland show *Nummer 28* and subsequent U.S. expansion in the same decade)
- The Facebook news feed (2006)
- YouTube stars (2010)
- YouTube Red (2015)
- YouTube TV (2017)
- Hyper-local reports on Instagram - e.g. OCInstanews on Instagram - See chapter on Uncle Tito (2010)

It's a story of *erosion of attention*. When TV and radio were young, there was very little competition for attention. By the time the internet blasted onto the scene, audiences were already fragmented. Now, with custom blogs, YouTube channels, and cable shows for every imaginable demographic, the big three networks will do just about anything to attract advertising dollars.

Questions for the kids: How many of you think it's interesting or even weird that your parents turn on this big TV and let a one-way broadcaster control what they're consuming every night and weekend? How many of you think it's weird that all the old people get together around these big sports events and treat it like it's the second coming?

It became a habit for a specific TV generation that grew up from about 1965 to 1995. That's all we had. When we were young, there was just CBS,

ABC, NBC, the Super Bowl, The World Series, the NBA Championships, the NCAA hoops tourney and the Stanley Cup. That was it. There were some more subtle events like Wimbledon, the Olympics every two to four years, the US Open, some big golf tournaments, and some horse races. . . but that was it. We were a tribe around a single camp fire.

Now, you've got five YouTube stars for every imaginable hobby, fetish and freak show out there. And, this is hell on advertisers. . . or possibly a boon. We've yet to really find out. You will hear all kinds of things about internet advertising – some true and some suspect – that inform us we're in a new age of customized or one-to-one advertising. But we've all seen the results of this. We were looking for some shoes and bought the pair we liked online, however we see ads for the same shoes follow us around the web for the following week. Initial reports claimed the Russians hacked the U.S. election by buying $100,000 worth of Facebook ads. Is that possible? Do Facebook ads work that well? If so, you'd see the big advertisers (think beer, insurance and pharma) dumping their large portions of their budgets into Facebook. But they're not. They're actually pulling back social media ad buy budgets (When Procter & Gamble Cut $200 Million in Digital Ad Spend, It Increased Its Reach 10% : http://bit.ly/2r28RET).

PROCTER GAMBLE
CUT DIGITAL
AD SPEND

There are a lot of moving parts in place. We'll talk more about this in an upcoming section.

The takeaways here are the following:

- Starbucks, Papa Johns, Toys 'R Us and lots of other companies know how to advertise online, on

- their own sites, via their publishing platforms, and in traditional media with native ads.
- News media and its delivery platforms have evolved from some very simple, centrally controlled, monopolistic networks to a hugely diverse, scattered mess that we witness today – for better or for worse.
- The dividing line (church and state) between network/local news coverage and advertising has never been more blurry. On the web it's perhaps worse.
- Targeted internet or digital advertising doesn't always work as well as claims profess.

Exercise: Watch the second half of a national nightly news cast (ABC, CBS or) on a Monday or Tuesday night. See if you can spot any native advertising in those second half of show content blocks (Content blocks are the segments between commercials - the 2nd half of show blocks contain more promotional content). If you have a DVR, back it up, whip out your phone and record it for us. We'll go over some of the good ones here in class NBC with the Chromecast. This works really well around holidays like Halloween, Valentine's Day, Christmas and Easter, but you'll find it all year long. If you want to get into full detective mode, you can dig into Google to see if the advertiser in question has ever bought regular break ads on that network in the past (even on different shows). Chances are they have, and they have an established relationship with the ad sales team at the network. Wink, wink. "How would you like some native editorial content in one of our TV shows (Today, GMA, Nightly News, etc.) as incentive for your next ad buy on our other shows like Modern Family, The Real Housewives and The Voice?"

What Is Transactional Journalism?

Earlier, we talked about how *humans* choose headlines, filter Facebook feeds (non-algorithm, human filters employed by Facebook), place stories "above the fold," and decide which press releases to run as news. The same applies to the generalized practice of journalism – reporting, scheduling interviews, gaining access to people, pulling sensitive information out of people and so forth. People are flawed, and their emotions, avarice, ambition and worldviews temper their actions in the day to day journalism world.

Enter "transactional journalism." Sharyl Attkisson's investigative journalism book called *The Smear: How Shady Political Operatives and Fake News Control What You See, What You Think, and How You Vote* popularized the term in recent times. For those of you who'd like to go deeper into 2016 election analysis, this book is an eye-opener.

Put simply, transactional journalism is just what it sounds like. Favors, access, money and influence are traded for articles, interviews, power-plays and the like. Even though journalism isn't the money-making machine it used to be thanks to the internet, there's still power to be wielded by transacting to gain favorable outcomes for yourself or unfavorable outcomes for your opponents or competitors.

In the middle of this power play sits the underpaid journalist whose only currency is often their ability to get stories onto the front pages or into the HuffPo. A reporter's career can turn on that coveted "scoop," so they're all motivated to beat their competitors to the punch when gaining access, information and secrets. That gives significant incentive to politicians, industry heads, bureaucrats, whistle-blowers, charlatans, and scammers that are interested in getting their messages across. They can trade direct access or even "off the record" info for favorable treatment, and many do this in a *quid pro quo* process all too familiar to Washington D.C. insiders. Of course, all kinds of people recognize the value of national and even local exposure for their causes, products, elections, gripes, vendettas and more. It's not just a D.C. phenomenon. It's just that the pros tend to operate there, where a lot of the money is.

So how does that look in specific day-to-day transactions between journalists and their information sources? There are all kinds of scenarios, including:

- A source might dictate publication timing as a condition for access
- A journalist might promise to ask specific questions while avoiding others
- A reporter could get too close to a source personally, thus jeopardizing their objectivity and opening them for favor requests (or demands!)
- A reporter might seek sources that align with their personal ideologies, thus benefiting the source and their own agenda

All sorts of other dilemmas – everything from blackmail to extortion – arise from this transactional orientation. It distorts the field of factual reporting while pressuring journalists to play games with sources in order to get the best coverage for their publications and accolades from their bosses.

In the past, journalists prided themselves on street smarts, persistence and logical deduction – all laudable traits for investigators following breaking news stories. However, the great reporter is the one with access to a "deep throat" or a Washington D.C. leaker from within one of the big three-letter agencies (CIA, FBI, DHS, NSA, DOD, DEA, State Department, etc.).

The flawed system creates an informational hierarchy in the press. Only those with goodies to trade get the stories first. Then poorer information or even misinformation trickles down to the poorly-placed or novice reporters down the rungs of the ladder. It works from both sides of the equation, too. Poor sources feed shoddy journalists.

In *The Smear*, Attkisson wrote:

"... this is a world in which little happens by

accident. Topics and people make news because it's all been prearranged, preplanned, agreed upon. More than ever, the sort of "reporting" conducted as a result of such efforts, both on the conservative and liberal sides, passes for news and is rewarded with clicks from readers and kudos from media managers. It's everything today's quasi-semi-news media seeks: quick, easy, low-cost, low-risk, requiring little effort and drawing lots of attention from the right people."

It's kind of depressing and all the more reason for you to become a more savvy media consumer. Attkisson is a highly decorated investigative journalist with a resume and reputation that's in many ways peerless in the modern age of internet journalism. Unfortunately, her type of journalism could be dying.

More on Native Advertising

"If it doesn't sell, it isn't creative."

– David Ogilvy

On the web, native advertising has been a huge success. In 2015, Scientific American magazine reported: "On NYTimes.com, readers spend as much time on the ads as on the articles." These are company-sponsored or, in some cases, NYTimes staff written articles that are designed to promote a product, brand, cause or service *and look like standard editorial within the publication.*

The Scientific American article goes on to note: "An Interactive Advertising Bureau study found that only 41 percent of general-news readers could tell such ads apart from real news stories." So the indication on the stories and links were so subtle that readers could not decipher editorial content from promoted advertisements on the web site.

Here's how blatantly ad-oriented the whole process is. The advertiser's "worry" is front and center while the reader's position is secondary.

The article continued: "Advertisers worry that the "Sponsored" label dissuades readers from clicking, so Web sites from NYTimes.com to BuzzFeed.com are making the labels smaller and less noticeable. Sometimes the labels disappear entirely."

How's that for deception? The publications – the New York Times no less! – no longer care about the clarity and transparency around fact and reportage. They just want their advertiser to not worry about that pesky sponsored label.

The native ad practice isn't just for broadcast news and print/web publications either. The article describes how the ads make their way into entertainment programming as well: "At a recent panel about the difficulty of advertising in the new, small-screen world, I heard an ad executive tell an impressive story. She had gotten a musical performance—paid for by her soft drink client—seamlessly inserted into a TV awards show, without any moment of blackness before or after. "It looked just like part of the real broadcast!" she recounted happily."

The story continued: "But how, then, could viewers tell the ad apart from independently produced material? A fellow panelist rolled his eyes. "Oh, good grief. People are savvy. They know!" he responded.

"But if advertisers truly believe in their material, they should have no problem labeling it as advertising. ("Sponsored post" is already a little vague; "From around the Web" and "More news you may like" are downright deceptive.)"

The full article is here: https://www.scientificamerican.com/article/truth-in-digital-advertising/

Every inch of the web, every broadcast and every news outlet is for sale. That's the common thread here. So, where you get your news matters, and how perceptive you are at spotting advertising vis a vis hard news is now a valuable skill (even though it shouldn't have to be).

Inside the Ad Buying Game

Earlier we talked about wink-wink advertising deals in the exercises. There's a subtle name for this particular in the industry. It's called "added value." The network or publisher will offer additional editorial and/or advertorial coverage of the company if there's a big ad buy at stake.

While the large networks like ABC, CBS, NBC and CNN typically avoid the practice in a *quid pro quo* manner, it's alive and well. They usually try to maintain their traditional "church and state" line between advertising and editorial, but in challenging ad markets (like the one we're in with all this internet disruption) almost every publisher and media concern will do nearly anything in order to secure the advertising business.

Here's a real life example from the magazine world. One of our partners in the media world (an ad broker/buyer) represented a client that wanted to purchase ads in eight different magazines. Every one of the magazines independently agreed to offer editorial coverage of the company in order to secure the deal. They settled on just three of the eight, but it was striking how all eight offered up what used to be a taboo exchange.

Brands Align with Causes and Emotional Campaigns

"The world is ruled and the destiny of civilization is established by the human emotions."

— Napoleon Hill

When brands, causes and products can't get immediate access to a purchasing customer or donor, they often try to attach to larger causes. There's a website, in fact, called Upworthy that designed its editorial with this idea in mind. Their approach is to sell big brands access and association with inspiring content that's shared across the web. That's their strategy in a nutshell.

Adweek described the arrangement in 2015 in an article titled <u>Emotional and Effective, Upworthy's Native Ads Have Brought in More Than $10 Million for the Site.</u>

http://bit.ly/2qZ5cYs

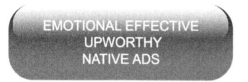

Some highlights:

> "Unilever svp of marketing Marc Mathieu said in a statement that, in less than eight months, Upworthy Collaborations got 175 million social impressions, 6 million social interactions and more than 15 million viewers. Most importantly, the brand reported a 17 percent increase in the perception the brand was committed to improving the future of the planet among those who saw its Upworthy content."

Unilever is one of the biggest consumer products conglomerates in the world. The content they originally published has since been taken down. The Adweek article details the goals and intent, however:

> "The branded content program . . . helps companies either by curating heartwarming and inspiring content created by the brand, working with the brand to create branded pieces or finding materials that align with the brand's mission and posting them on behalf of the brand. The content is then promoted on Upworthy's

site and on social, and boosting online chatter through #UpChats on Twitter."

Who else was purchasing Upworthy campaigns in 2015?

- Toms shoes
- Whirlpool
- Gap
- Holiday Inn
- Pantene
- Dove
- A&E
- Universal Pictures
- Virgin Mobile
- American Family Insurance
- CoverGirl
- The Bill & Melinda Gates Foundation
- The United Nations
- The U.S. Fund for UNICEF

The article goes on to say that "Toms reported a 69 percent higher monthly social media growth during the time its campaigns ran with Upworthy." That's pretty good ROI on exposure.

And just for some flavor, here's a Starbucks video (noted in the article) that was produced by Upworthy Collaborations: http://bit.ly/2r0q41r

It's about a deaf woman who finds a community of other deaf people at her local Starbucks.

WHEN WE *get* TOGETHER

2:43 / 2:45

While I don't want to get too cynical here since the story is a legitimately touching one, I'd like to note a few points:

1. This is a nicely done albeit generic piece that evokes a very happy and uplifting emotional state in the viewer. There's just not a lot of detail in it. It works, but it's thin.
2. It promotes the idea that community and gathering in person is a positive thing. Who can argue with that? The tagline at the end sums it up: "Good things happen when we get together."
3. A critical viewer, however, might wonder why this 25+ or 30+ year-old woman (by appearances) is only now finding friends to do sign language with. That's a little odd. It took Starbucks to get her together with people of the same predicament? It's odd but forgivable.

The point is that this stuff works. It could be fake, staged, pre-planned and strategized in detail, but it works. The social media numbers climb, the impressions rack up, and the brands get favorable exposure.

Comedians as News Sources

> "The human race has only one really effective weapon, and that is laughter. The moment it arises, all our hardnesses yield, all our irritations and resentments slip away and a sunny spirit takes their place."
>
> — Mark Twain

As the news developed into something resembling sports commentary or reality entertainment in the late 1990's and early 2000's, news analysis became vital to TV ratings on both cable and traditional broadcast outlets. You can read more about this transition from news to entertainment here (CNN Had a Problem. Donald Trump Solved It. Inside the strange symbiosis between Jeff Zucker and the president he helped create. BY JONATHAN MAHLER APRIL 4, 2017): https://nyti.ms/2r2aW3F

CNN PROBLEM
DONALD TRUMP
SOLVED

Basically, Jeff Zucker moved from NBC entertainment in late 1980's, 1990's and early 2000's (1988 Olympics, *Friends* sit-com, *Fear Factor* reality TV, and Donald Trump's *The Apprentice)* to head of *CNN Worldwide* in 2013, bringing with him all he learned about sports programming, entertainment ratings, and late night comedy/interview formats to the field of news production at CNN.

As entertainment, drama, hyperbole and hype took over, other entertainers took notice. Some of the early beginnings could be traced back to Comedy Central's *The Daily Show with Craig Kilborn*. Even earlier news analysis could be traced back as far as Lenny Bruce, George Carlin and Robin Williams – all comedians with a political or social edge to their acts.

Craig Kilborn's show on Comedy Central was somewhat pioneering. It was political satire played out as if it was a live news read. *Comedy* – with all the license the writers, directors, producers and talent could possibly take with the material. Unlike "real news" it could easily skew facts to fit a comic gag.

Interestingly, Kilborn previously anchored sports coverage on the comedically emerging ESPN. That network's SportsCenter show used to be somewhat funny and sarcastic with a whole slew of anchors like Kilborn joking about plays of the day and inserting their own comedic personalities into the show. Later on, there was even a network sitcom on ABC called *Sports Night* that aired from 1998 to 2000. The show chronicled the early days of a fictitious ESPN-like network. More interesting stuff from Wikipedia:

> "The show is said to be a semi-fictional account of the ESPN SportsCenter team of Keith Olbermann and Dan Patrick, with Rydell representing Olbermann and McCall representing Patrick. Patrick has confirmed this on his syndicated radio program The Dan Patrick Show. It has also been said that many of the story lines for Casey McCall were inspired by Craig Kilborn, who was an anchor on *SportsCenter* during the mid-1990s."

So Kilborn was an early comedic act to come out of sports. He'd go on the pioneer *The Daily Show,* which is now a modern staple for all kinds of people who'd prefer to get their politics from a comedy show as opposed to a stuffy or angry conventional outlet like CNN or Fox News. Interestingly, Keith Olbermann went on to host his own political show on MSNBC, then another political show on Al Gore's *Current TV*. Perhaps more interesting, in 2013 *Current TV* was sold to *Al Jazeera*, one of the alternative networks we'll examine later.

Now, back to *The Daily Show*. Steven Colbert of Comedy Central's *The Colbert Report,* was one of the original on-air contributors to Craig Kilborn's and John Stewart's *Daily Shows*. Colbert is regarded as a big political commentator these days, albeit via comedy. Trevor Noah succeeded John Stewart as the host of the show in 2015. Like Colbert, he started out as a contributor to the show. Like Kilborn, Olbermann, and Stewart, Noah was the furthest thing from an experienced journalist. He was an actor and a comedian from South Africa.

In any event, these shows are important, because these days a significant portion of the population gets their news from shows like *The Daily Show, The Onion* and the various clips they spawn on YouTube. According to Pew Research, "One-in-ten (10%) online adults said they got news from the [*The Colbert Report*] in the previous week, on par with such sources as the Wall Street Journal and USA Today." (December 2014 study) In 2015, <u>Pew Research cited that same 2014 survey</u> and found that 12% of online Americans got their news from *The Daily Show. The Onion* is another satire/comedy publisher on the web.

Here are those two links: <u>https://pewrsr.ch/2r0CHtl</u> and <u>https://pewrsr.ch/2r0h2BP</u>

Some of the others personalities that have political influence on large portions of the population include:

- Seth Meyers (comedian – started on SNL)
- Jimmy Kimmel (comic actor and sketch producer for radio – started on Los Angeles radio station KROQ)
- Jimmy Fallon (comedian/musician – started on SNL)
- Dennis Miller (comedian – started on SNL)
- Tina Fey (comedian/actress/writer – started on SNL)
- Sarah Silverman (comedian/actress, also girlfriend/partner of Kimmel from 2002-2009)

The general issue here is that a large portion of the population – who knows how many get clips shared via phones, tablets and laptops – consumes news via characters that are somewhat fictional and are certainly not trained journalists. You might even inquire as to whether any of the people mentioned above have college degrees.

While the viewers of these shows may consume news elsewhere, there's a chance they don't. And there's a chance the shows form their major opinions about how the world works and who's responsible for what. *And,* there's ample research showing that the emotional reach of comedy allows speakers and performers of all kinds to make indelible impressions on their audiences – much more so than people that are delivering straight, dry news accounts that appear on traditional, non-comedy media.

Oh, and so you don't have to, we looked up the colleges and degrees of the people mentioned above. Here you go. You're welcome:

- Craig Kilborn – Montana State University (no major given on Wikipedia)
- John Stewart – College of William & Mary (psychology major)
- Keith Olbermann – Cornell University (communication arts)
- Stephen Colbert – Northwestern University (theater)
- Trevor Noah – none listed (looks like he went directly into soap opera acting and comedy after attending a private catholic elementary and high school in Johannesburg)
- Seth Meyers – Northwestern University (none listed)
- Jimmy Kimmel – Arizona State University (looks like he never graduated)
- Jimmy Fallon – College of Saint Rose, Albany, New York (communications – he completed the degree in 2009, 14 years after leaving to pursue comedy career)
- Dennis Miller – Point Park University, Pittsburgh, Pennsylvania (journalism)
- Tina Fey – University of Virginia (drama)
- Sarah Silverman – New York University (studied for one year, didn't graduate)

These are all people that had clear intentions of working in show business but somehow ended up influencing voters all across the U.S. for decades and decades to come. Interestingly, they started in either sports broadcasting or comedy and eventually found their way into politics. You'll see all of these people – with the exceptions of Kilborn and Fallon – wade heavily into the drama, passion and shrillness of national and international politics if you take a quick spin through YouTube and combine any controversial issue with their names.

With the Internet, You Can Believe Whatever You Want

In the days prior to the internet, there were not nearly as many media outlets, opinions and publications as there are today. Libraries were full of all kinds of differing opinion, fact and reporting, but not many people outside of college students and professors researching papers got into it much. University libraries used to pride themselves on the extent of their physical resources.

But you couldn't universally search a library from a keyboard. You had to wade through microfiche and microfilm or pore over texts to find what you were looking for. These days, you've got access to petabytes of information via keyword search. Anything is yours in nanoseconds.

That essentially means you can believe anything you want and have plenty of other kooks (or even smart people) backing it up with "facts," proof and convincing blog and vlog entries.

One of your primary objectives as students is to see through this and form your own opinions based on sound analysis, common sense, physics, math, statistics, intuition, your command of the English language and other skills you've picked up along the way.

As you come across people with diverse ideas and differing viewpoints, remember this. There's a lot of hooey out there, and there are plenty of facts to back it up. In subjective fields like politics, it's even scarier, because there's a lot of power at stake. Same goes for consumer advertising. Trillions of dollars are spent trying to part you from your money. *It's your job to understand what's being sold.*

Geo-fencing and Ad Tracking

Our houses and phones are filled with fun digital technology. It can get a little weird, however, when advertising seems to be following us around on the web and in our pockets. Some people have reported sneezing and talking about sickness then discovering ads for cold medicines in their web pages. Others shop for shoes and find their feeds inundated with complementary fashions.

And, a lot of the time it doesn't seem to work that well. I'm continuously followed around by eyeglass ads months after I originally purchased a pair . . . *online, from the company I bought them from!*

If you track some of this stuff, you might think:

- Is Alexa (Amazon Echo) listening to my conversations?
- Did Facebook turn on my phone microphone and spy on me?
- Are these machines reading my mind?

It can definitely seem that way. Joanna Stern of the Wall Street Journal investigated these suspicions.

https://on.wsj.com/2qZwxd3

WSJ JOANNA STERN
FACEBOOK
SPYING

Here's the breakdown for our purposes (with some additional insights):

Facebook and Alexa don't listen to us. Storing and analyzing language from huge amounts of audio data is not technically possible at this stage of the game. Amazon doesn't do this, and neither do Facebook, Instagram or Snapchat.

These companies do have other ways of triangulating purchasing behavior both online and offline. As Stern notes, when you use loyalty cards at markets and drug stores, that data is shared with companies like Facebook. So, if you purchase cold medicine at Rite Aid (a drug store chain), Facebook, Amazon and the rest find out. Actually, those platforms technically facilitate advertisers who find out. It's the advertisers that get the ball rolling.

This is verbatim from Stern's article:

> "Information about the contents of my shopping bag began to spread. A third-party data collector—likely Nielsen-Catalina Solutions—added it to the purchase history it acquires from Walgreens.
> "Johnson & Johnson, maker of Sudafed, paid the data broker for that information. With the use of Facebook's tools, the information from my loyalty card—email, phone number, etc.—was

matched with my Facebook account. (Data brokers run personal information through an algorithm before uploading so it's not identifiable, Facebook says, but it still can be matched with Facebook account information.)

"Then via Facebook, Johnson & Johnson decided to target adults ages 25 to 54 who bought Sudafed or a competing brand. In other words, me."

Pretty crafty, right? It appears to be mind reading, as if Stern mentioned her cold or cough into Alexa. But it's really just data triangulation the shopper opted into. Her article shows you how to turn off these advertising triangulation capabilities via the social networks.

Something called geofencing also plays a role. When you wander around town, places you visit contain wi-fi networks and/or beacons attached to RFID or your phone's internal GPS system

> **Geofencing:** the use of GPS or RFID technology to create a virtual geographic boundary, enabling software to trigger a response when a mobile device enters or leaves a particular area.

(if you have it turned on). Most people have GPS turned on to navigate traffic and so forth. So, if you're on a car lot shopping for a new automobile, that information can be sent to advertisers who'd like to push you notifications about car sales around town. It can seem like mind reading, but it's just simple deduction and geo-targeting. They know where you are, so they can serve up relevant ads based on your location and an assumption about what you're doing there. Apps like Facebook, Twitter, Instagram and Snapchat usually have "push notifications" turned on by default, so they can send you advertising messages or embed them into your feed based on your geographical behaviors. If you're at a sporting event, they might feed you beer ads. If you're getting a haircut, they might send you a Super Cuts coupon for the next time around. The possibilities are endless.

There's a third angle here, too. Facebook Pixel is a relatively old technology that allows advertisers to track your behavior as you cruise around the web. Millions of websites and apps use a single pixel installed on their pages to understand when you hit their pages, how long you stay, and something about what you do (think conversion, where you buy something or download something before leaving the site). These are all-purpose trackers that can triangulate data with geofencing and loyalty card data in order to deliver more relevant offers and products to you as you cruise around the web and use your mobile devices in the real world.

It's all legal, and you're able to turn some of it off. Check Stern's article for instructions on that.

All of this stuff is correlated with posts you've liked, things you click on, friends you have, things you retweet and so on. Your public profile is developed in more and more detail the longer you use the web and apps (apps are really just the web, by the way). Google AdWords and the various technologies of that platform do the same things, and they may be sharing data with Nielsen, Amazon, Facebook and the rest. As consumers, we don't get much insight into those data sharing agreements.

> **Push notification:** a message that pops up on a mobile device. App publishers can send them at any time; users don't have to be in the app or using their devices to receive them.

Anyway, you're being tracked, your habits are known, and the big web technology platforms are constantly trying to perfect this stuff. You've been warned. It's neither good nor bad until something bad comes of it. Could your shopping habits flag you for a *Minority Report*-style "pre-crime?" That's where the larger ethical challenges lie. *Minority Report* is the book by Philip K. Dick (1956) which was made into a movie starring Tom Cruise in 2002. The plot describes the conflict between government and citizens when crimes can be predicted before they occur.

Broken Web: Advertising and Ad Blocker Turn Off Requests

Since we're on the web ads topic, let's ponder what's breaking the web – namely, ad-blocker subversion. These things are annoying, and they prevent you from quickly accessing the articles, videos, audio and other content that you'd like to peruse. If you put on your advertiser/media lens, however, you can see what's up. There's a war afoot.

There's a war going on in your computer, on your browser, and over the web. It's a funny thing, because sometimes it's a battle between one Google division and another. It's about what you can and can't see on the internet. Google AdWords and AdSense want businesses to purchase ads and people to consume ads that are placed within the Google search universe and embedded into web pages. They want consumers to see ads that are relevant to the searches they perform and the sites they visit. By the way, there are all kinds of other advertising platforms out there (DoubleClick, Adobe, Kenshoo, Marin, IgnitionOne, etc.), however, and they compete for eyeballs and clicks with Google. Facebook, Twitter, Snapchat and other social media platforms are also competing for the same eyeballs.

All these platforms integrate with media, news, entertainment, how-to, video, and other content sites. Every web publisher that's interested in making a buck wants to monetize via these advertising platforms.

Interestingly, ad blocking software thwarts a lot of this advertising.

If you have an ad blocker installed in your browser (I have AdBlock installed on Google Chrome), you've probably noticed that news sites in particular want you to turn off that blocker on their sites so they can serve up ads freely. Lately, these sites are sampling your browser, noticing that you're running something like AdBlock, and then requesting that you disable the ad blocker for their site. They want to be able to charge their advertisers for unfettered access to the people who traffic their articles, videos, audio and other content. It's understandable. A site like Fortune or the New York Times can't make money if they can't sell advertising in the places where consumers are huddling up and reading/watching/listening.

So they want you to turn off ad blocking on their sites. Their IT people have figured out how to notice your ad blocker and interrupt your web surfing.

Google, on the other hand, wants its users to have a good experience with the Chrome browser while serving up its own competitive ads. They're in a weird place. One division wants to make the browsing experience good, while the other is competing for advertising dollars. Google would love to block ads via Chrome (new ad blocking features have just been released, in fact - http://bit.ly/2r1dQ8K).

This approach could allow them to eliminate the competition they choose.

The problem is that a lot of those same advertisers are buying on other platforms plus Google AdWords. Google doesn't want to alienate them. But at the same time, they don't want to cripple the browsing experience for Chrome users.

It's pretty crazy stuff. In the end, however, web/browser/app users suffer because ad-blocking disable scripts are downright annoying. They're breaking the web!

Here's the glaring issue. *Web publications, web content producers and media developers that need to distribute content via the web cannot make money with the current state of things!* There's just too much good content out there, and audiences are so fragmented that they're finding their own "long tail" fun in the most unpredictable of places. There is no longer a network triumvirate – ABC, CBS and NBC. There are no monopolies on the channels. It's open season, and the only people winning are the social media platforms and the ad buyers/ad platforms. Advertisers are subject to click-bots and all kinds of other shenanigans that we'll get into later. They have no clear idea about which ads are working and on which platforms. It's a crazy game, and the cost of entry is really cheap. Of course, you can Tweet and gain attention for $0 if you have a decent following.

This from Sharyl Attkisson's *The Smear:*

> *The past two decades have served as an ideal incubator for an industry of smears and fake news. The tools and tactics have evolved from old-school to high-tech. Incredible amounts of money change hands, yet some of the most damaging smears can be accomplished with little more than an idea and an Internet connection. By 2016, a Pew Research Center report found more than 44 percent of the American adult population got its news on Facebook, which had 1.09 billion active daily users. Some of that news is true. Some of it's not. Today, an entire movement can be started with a few bogus Twitter accounts and 140 characters or less. "You don't have to spend millions on political ad buys anymore," observes one operative in the business. "You can spark wildfires with just a tiny little stick now, which is a new thing."*

> **Long Tail:** (in retail and marketing) used to refer to the large number of products that sell in small quantities, as contrasted with the small number of best-selling products.

Ad Bots and Suckered Advertisers

Do you ever catch yourself wondering why or how an Instagram account you came across has so many likes, comments and followers? You ask yourself if they've purchased that traffic or if it's legit.

Multiply that feeling times a trillion, and you've got the current scandal going on in the backrooms of online advertising boardrooms. There's a huge scam afoot, and not many people are discussing it in the inter-webs.

Oxford Biochronometrics chronicled the issue in their 2015 report, Quantifying Online Advertising Fraud: Ad-Click Bots vs Humans. It's a fascinating read about how ads perform across the internet and if real humans are actually seeing them.

http://bit.ly/2HqTwce

QUANTIFYING
ONLINE
ADVERTISING FRAUD

Their research set out to determine the ratio of ad-clicks that are human initiated as opposed to automated by a computer program (bot or script that crawls the internet).

Here are some highlights:

> "Later, in December, Google made a similar announcement when it stated that its research has showed that 56.1 per cent of ads served on the Internet are never "in view.""

What is a bot?
According to Oxford Biochronometrics, a bot is "a software application that runs automated tasks over the Internet. . . bots perform tasks that are both simple and structurally repetitive, at a much higher rate than would be possible for a human alone."

"eBay has been to court in an attempt to suppress a third-party company from using bots to traverse their site looking for bargains; this approach backfired on eBay and attracted the attention of further bots."

"Bot farms are known to be used in online app stores, like the Apple App Store and Google Play, to manipulate positions or to increase positive ratings/reviews while another, more malicious use of bots is in the coordination and operation of an automated attack on networked computers, such as a denial-of-service attack by a botnet."

"Internet bots can also be used to commit click fraud and more recently have seen usage around Massively Multiplayer Online Roleplaying Games (MMORPG) as computer game bots."

"A spambot is an internet bot that attempts to spam large amounts of content on the Internet, usually adding advertising links."

"Bots are also used to buy up good seats for concerts, particularly by ticket brokers who resell the tickets. Bots are employed against entertainment event-ticketing sites, like TicketMaster.com. The bots are used by ticket brokers to unfairly obtain the best seats for themselves while depriving the general public from also having a chance to obtain the good seats. The bot runs through the purchase process and obtains better seats by pulling as many seats back as it can."

"Bots are also used to artificially increase views for

YouTube videos. Bots are used to increase traffic counts on analytics reporting to extract money from advertisers. A study by comScore found that 54 percent of display ads shown in thousands of campaigns between May 2012 and February 2013 never appeared in front of a human being."

"In 2012 reporter Percy Lipinski reported that he discovered millions of bot or botted or pinged views at CNN iReport. CNN iReport quietly removed millions of views from the account of so-called superstar iReporter Chris Morrow. A followup investigation lead to a story published on the citizen journalist platform, Allvoices. It is not known if the ad revenue received by CNN from the fake views was ever returned to the advertisers."

HERE'S THE WHOPPER CONCLUSION FROM THE REPORT

". . . at best, 88 percent of the ad-clicks were made by bots on the LinkedIn platform while at worst 98 percent were from bots on the Google ad platform."

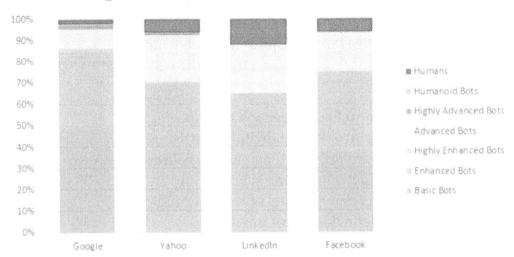

Figure 1: Ratio of Ad-Bot Clicks to Human Clicks

Legend:
- Humans
- Humanoid Bots
- Highly Advanced Bots
- Advanced Bots
- Highly Enhanced Bots
- Enhanced Bots
- Basic Bots

More scandalous details:

> "There were no instances where we were not charged for an ad-click that was made by any type of bot."

> Their conclusion: "There are perhaps few industries where overcharging on such a scale as demonstrated here would be tolerated, but until very recently, the ability to model both human and bot behaviour at the necessary level of complexity (and thus hold advertising platforms to account) was not commercially feasible."

Ad Bot Update

The previous section about bots came from data studied in 2012 and 2013. You might wonder if things have improved since then. That doesn't appear to be the case. *The Wall Street Journal's* latest take on the issue, "The Internet's 'Original Sin' Endangers More Than Privacy," show how troubles have compounded. We've clipped heavily from the original source here.

> "The problem began with what some call the internet's original sin—offering free software and content in exchange for the hope of unprecedented growth. Advertising was supposed to pay the way."

> "The plan worked well for Facebook and Google, which together control 87% of digital advertising, according to Bloomberg. But their success belies a basic truth: Internet advertising is broken. It abuses users, starves publishers of revenue, and creates unprecedented levels of fraud for advertisers. The situation drove Procter & Gamble's chief brand officer to declare last year that "the days of giving digital [advertising] a pass are over.""

> "Internet advertising started simply, but over time organically evolved a mess of middle players and congealed into a surveillance economy. Today, between end users, publishers and advertisers stand a throng of agencies, trading desks, demand side platforms, network exchanges and yield optimizers. Intermediaries track users in an attempt to improve revenue."

This is where the bots and clicks can be gamed and where a lot of advertising fraud lies. The article continues:

> "When you visit the celebrity website TMZ, for instance, you face as many as 124 trackers, according to a Crownpeak test. Your data is stored and profiled to retarget promotions that shadow

you around the Internet. You become the product."

"The Facebook-Google ad duopoly also vacuums up gigabytes of personal data: Google collects the places you've gone, devices you've used, everything you've searched or browsed, pictures of your children, emails, contacts and more. Facebook knows where you logged on and has access to webcams and microphones, emails, messages, call logs and more."

"The inconveniences go beyond privacy. Studies show that as much as half the data consumed on mobile plans goes to downloading ads and trackers, adding significantly to fixed mobile data plans. The sheer scale of material adds at least five seconds to mobile page load times, according to the New York Times. As much as 50% of mobile battery life is consumed by ads while browsing."

"Publishers have not fared much better in their Faustian bargain of exchanging digital content for the hope of better distribution and revenue from the duopoly. Newspapers have been particularly hard hit, with total ad revenues dropping from $49 billion in 2006 to $18 billion in 2016. About 96% of all growth in digital ad spend went to Google and Facebook last year according to Zenith."

". . . ad fraud will reach $19 billion in 2018, or about $51 million a day, according to Juniper research."

The entire article, written by the CEO of the Brave browser, which is a novel solution to the problem, is here: https://on.wsj.com/2r9W1Va

Advertising Via "Thought Leaders"

"Ours has become a world where a tragic number of people have become more fascinated by materialism and the lives of distant narcissists than by their own life experience."

– Brendon Burchard

If you can gain significant attention by Tweeting, Instagramming or Facebooking to a large population of like-minded people, you have what makes for an advertising solution or an advertising platform.

You may have come across this already. It works quite well on both large scale and small scale social media accounts. The concept involves influence peddling and micro-payments.

Here's how it works in the art world on Instagram. Artists that desire more exposure set up business accounts on Instagram. They start following other artists and museum goers, and hashtagging their works with the conventional tags like: #oilpainting, #art, #iloveart, #instaart, #inspiration, #fineart and so on.

There's a subgroup of Instagrammers who promote and curate art on the platform. These accounts inevitably figure out who the emerging and newly exposed artists are. They follow artists and comment and like their posts. Eventually these curators message or comment on the artist's posts, telling them that they can be featured on the curator's Instagram page for a fee (details in their bio). The bio usually contains a link to an e-commerce site where the artist can purchase exposure in the curated feed for micro-payments.

Here's an example:

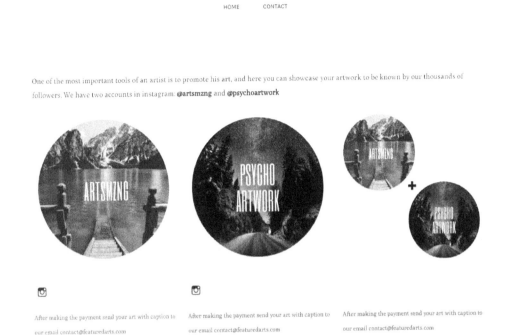

This is going on all over the world. Imagine the vigorish that changes hands on larger trafficked sites. @psychoartwork had almost 32,000 followers as of this printing. Some of those should are fairly targeted art lovers, as you can imagine.

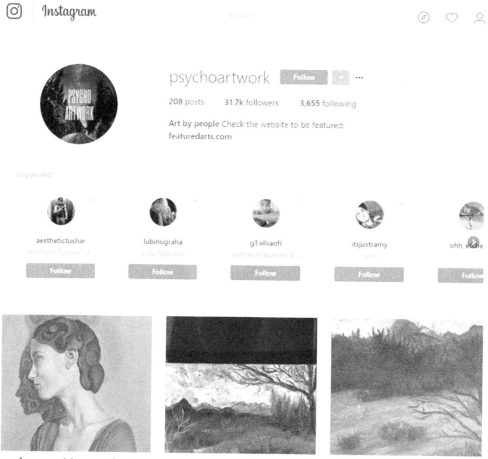

https://www.instagram.com/psychoartwork

Now, imagine what a Kardashian can pull in by showing off a purse or some fashion outfit or skin cream? (Kim Kardashian West has 109,000,000 followers as of 2018!) Direct promotions via those accounts have to be supremely lucrative. The transactions for publicity and promotion for those types of sites are often handled by traditional media buyers, agents and ad agencies.

This is the kind of cross-pollination advertising that is contributing to the breakdown of traditional media channels. One post by Kardashian in one day gets 2.1 million likes and almost 30,000 comments. That one post – just a photo! – is reaching more people than many primetime cable TV shows that last a half hour. One day on her account (if she posts four times) gathers up more eyeballs and engagement than all the cable news channels combined. These are people commenting and engaging with the post. The potential reach is 109 million people, and the ones interacting with the posts are consistently in the 1.5 million to 2 million range (likes).

It's worth mentioning again. People – especially the young ones – are constantly on the "black mirrors." That's the new TV, and advertisers have been exploiting these new platforms for years.

Case Study: Who is Uncle Tito?

My older sons (13 and 15) have been following people on Instagram for a couple of years now. One of the first guys they glommed onto in a celebrity kind of way was someone who referred to himself as Uncle Tito. This is a surf industry guy, about 32 years old, who's hyper focused on the local scene here in Newport Beach. He frequents the same coffee shop, bashes on Starbucks, visits lifeguards, berates road bicyclists he's dubbed "butt darts," eats at local banzai bowl shops, and drops in on local surf industry offices in Huntington Beach, Costa Mesa, Newport Beach and elsewhere.

He has a 19K following of mostly young kids (TARGETED market!) and is very engaging with his posts. Almost everything is in video snippet or "story" form. He was one of the first people I saw who truly understood and exploited the story feature on Instagram.

Here's his profile:

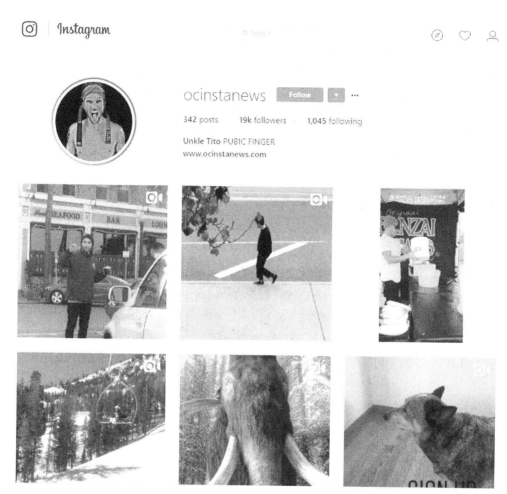

https://www.instagram.com/ocinstanews

Looks like he was at Mammoth Mountain recently for some skiing. It wouldn't surprise me if he got some $$$ to head up there and cover the slopes.

In any event, you can see how micro-targeted brands can reach very distinct audiences with all the kinds of fun and games they like watching, eating and doing (think surf, ski, coffee, gourmet eats). There are thousands of these influencers in every imaginable nook and cranny of the country, and some of them are making money via advertising (either native ads or in-your-face traditional promotions).

The lines between mediums continue to blur, and the

traditional/conventional channels continue to eat the dust of the new social platforms. That last bit should have a little more qualification. Certainly, the big ad agencies, celebrities and brands are leveraging social media. However, these little micro-markets are fascinating, and the profits often go directly to the micro-celebrities.

What is Janrain, and Why Should You Care About It?

If you've ever logged into a new site using your Facebook, Google, Twitter or LinkedIn credentials, you may have used Janrain or something similar. The product is transparent to users, but it creates a login account on participating sites. The technology behind it is called OpenID.

It's an easy way for users to skip making up a new login and password for every ecommerce, news or other web site they want to use. While Janrain pulls emails, phone numbers and other social media data from your social media accounts to establish logins, it's not completely clear how much of that information is used for other purposes.

According to Wikipedia, "It uses profile data, such as a user's age, gender, interests, and location, allowing marketers to target advertising messages."

So, there's more than meets the eye here. The technology does make it simpler and faster for users that want to take some shortcuts, however that may come at some cost to privacy.

In these days of Facebook paranoia, fake news scandals, Russian hacking claims and other privacy concerns, it's surprising a company like Janrain hasn't gathered up its share of negative news headlines. Their business model and wide reach across the web make them an easy target for criticism.

Part 5 – Follow the Money: Major, Mainstream Advertising

Why does the news industry exist?

In the news business, there's a symbiotic relationship between audience and publisher. A publisher needs to retain its audience while accomplishing specific goals with respect to advertisers and business constituents. Those goals generally involve selling a product, service or cause.

Generally, the news audience thinks they're getting a bunch of free cool stuff – free news programming in the case of broadcast TV over the FCC airwaves and $100-200/month in the case of cable TV. Essentially they're being informed, entertained and emotionally engaged then interrupted with advertisements.

If the news story is about health, people tend to personalize it. If it's local and relevant to their lives and the people they know, all the better

The emotional power of the story is what keeps people engaged. We tend to think that we're rational, level-headed and calm when we gather our information. Countless studies prove the opposite, however. Read any of the popular psychology texts from the last 20 years, and you'll stumble across this consistent finding – *people make emotional decisions first, then they gather information which supports that decision.* The same phenomenon occurs with news. People read a story with the intent of being informed – as if they're going to base some rational decisions on the information, like picking a stock, buying bitcoin, voting on a candidate, or making travel plans – then they'll fall back to their already-established emotional decision, only using the news to support that previously established stance.

People also follow current news to conform to the tribe. They want to have something interesting to talk about. It's a big motivator. People want to appear knowledgeable and fit in with their peers.

In any event, the publisher's main goal (whether it's a YouTube channel or a conventional newspaper) is to match content choices with the goals, fears, aspirations and previously-established storylines of its audience. The Wall Street Journal has to tailor a more conservative story to its audience and deliver editorial themes that reflect that orientation, although that publication also includes OpEds that stray from conservative viewpoints. Same with the Huffington Post – but it's liberal in its bias.

In the news business, publishers deliver this content around several general categories, which include:

- o Sports teams
- o Weather
- o Business and economics
- o Arts & Entertainment (including books, games, pop culture, celebrity gossip, movies and plays)
- o Restaurants and food (this could be considered an arts & entertainment sub-category)
- o Community gossip, events and happenings (the community can be the world, nation, state or town)
- o Technology (this could be considered a business sub-category)
- o Politics, voting and legislation
- o War/conflict developments
- o Crime, tragedy and scandal events

The audience comes into this news universe in a number of ways. They may find time to check social network news via Facebook. They might pull up a favorite news site at set times during the day. They might hear something on the radio then research it further on the internet. They could see a meme on Instagram and look up the keywords to figure out what it's about and get in on the joke. There are a million ways in.

The publisher's goal (if they're using advertising as a business model) is to match audience fears and desires with the right news, then transition that audience into relevant advertising.

Here's a case study of this concept in action from a "news" site that has a highly targeted audience with very tightly defined aspirations and fears.

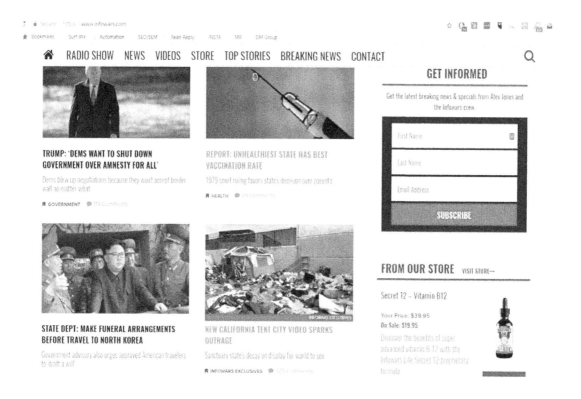

This is the Alex Jones site InfoWars, which arguably has an audience of conspiracy theory-inclined people. The stories on the left stoke fears about immigration, vaccination risks, travel fears and homelessness. The ad in this particular frame promotes a vitamin B12 supplement, which is one way for the fearful reader to take back some control in their life. They can manage their health with something within their own personal control, all while worrying about this disintegrating, fear-inducing world described on the left.

If you look at the other advertisements on the site, you'll find immunity enhancers, male potency and vitality supplements, water filtration systems, survival foods, seeds, privacy and security systems, radios (for communicating when the internet goes down), outdoor survival gear, radiation and nuclear holocaust survival tools, and a full array of books that relate to these topics. You can buy all of these products on the site, and they're all products that, in a way, solve the issues stirred up by the fear and insecurity developed by the predominant news stories and analysis on the site.

Here's an example from a politically liberal site called Daily Kos.

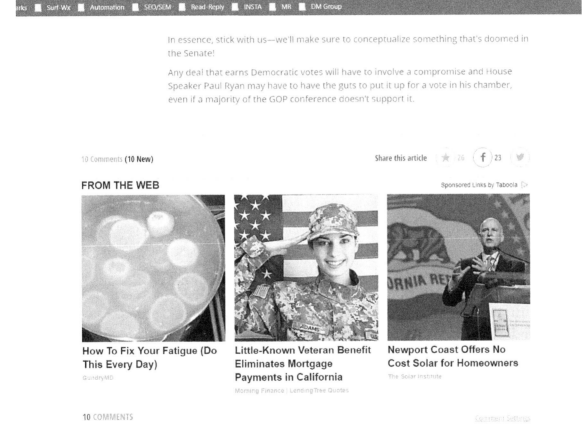

In essence, stick with us—we'll make sure to conceptualize something that's doomed in the Senate!

Any deal that earns Democratic votes will have to involve a compromise and House Speaker Paul Ryan may have to have the guts to put it up for a vote in his chamber, even if a majority of the GOP conference doesn't support it.

10 Comments (**10 New**)   Share this article   ★ 26 f 23

FROM THE WEB   Sponsored Links by Taboola

How To Fix Your Fatigue (Do This Every Day)
GundryMD

Little-Known Veteran Benefit Eliminates Mortgage Payments in California
Morning Finance | LendingTree Quotes

Newport Coast Offers No Cost Solar for Homeowners
The Solar Institute

10 COMMENTS   Comment Settings

The article is about immigration and the DACA deal. It provokes fear and outrage amongst its liberal readers, conditions that are deleterious to health and sanity, of course.

The solution? Offer ads that help combat fatigue via diet, solve financial problems by eliminating mortgage payments, and solving energy issues with solar power. One of the interesting things about these ads is that they're positioned as news articles (remember the talk earlier about Ogilvy and his ads that look like editorial?). If you click on the article titles, however, you're sent to "squeeze pages" pages that are really nothing more than an advertisement. One is a video squeeze pages framed as education, the other two are actual text squeeze pages that send you to lead generation forms, where you insert your email address to get more information. We'll talk more about squeeze pages and how to identify them in Part 6.

The general point here is that the state of the audience is crucial to the message of the advertising. Think about it. If you're relaxing and watching football on the weekend, you're susceptible to messages about delicious food and beer (as well as those non-aspirational but fear-induced messages about male virility). If you're hell-bent on impending Armageddon on a Monday at the office, then you're more likely to connect with messages about firearms and security devices.

With traditional news media like the nightly TV news, viewing times play a role. These programs often happen around family time, meal time, travel time and community time. We share in the horror, dismay, hope and despair of the news programming. We discuss over dinner. We form views. We prioritize. What we don't quite realize, however, is that the TV, radio, YouTube and the rest are shaping that prioritization and view formation. They choose what we pay attention to in a sense. In the case of YouTube, this may be

> **". . mainstream media is a billion-dollar business that is created and operated as a conduit to sell products, not to inform you.** The advertisers and corporations call the shots. Everything else is window dressing. You may as well **get your news from a Macy's clerk."**
>
> John C. Dvorak, Technology Journalist and Co-Host of the *No Agenda Show* Podcast

less so. Like Facebook, YouTube does, however, learn from viewers and present news and views based on prior likes, follows, subscribes and video views.

If we take a step back and consider things from the perspective of the advertiser and the media/publisher, we can see with a little more clarity.

Think about the "state of the audience" as if you were a news show, an advertiser or a ratings company (like Nielsen or SoundScan). Things are fairly simple from where they're standing. They want audiences that are experiencing specific states. We can divide these states into three general categories – body, mind and spirit.

Body
- Hungry
- Stressed
- Fearful
- Tired
- Worried about health
- Worried about personal safety
- Worried about privacy, hackers, personal secrets
- Worried about safety of public/nation/community

Mind

- Worried about the children, grandchildren, foreign hungry children
- Worried about what they can do, how they can vote, weapons they can use
- Figuring out how to make money, save money, protect money, spend money wisely

Spirit
- Dejected
- Hopeless

- Searching
- Scared
- Anxious
- Nervous
- Suspicious
- Cynical
- Hopeful
- Altruistic
- Generous
- Aspiring for something/someone/somewhere/somehow

The nightly news finds these audience states every night. Some might argue that they create these states every evening. Again, the shows air around dinner time when families are together and can reinforce dogmas, philosophies, gripes, grievances and so forth. They show prominently in airports (where CNN dominates the screens), restaurants and bars, where people are in states of agitation, nervousness and general malaise. Nowadays news follows us around 24x7 since CNN, Fox, MSNBC et al have become cable mainstays.

In the next section, we'll move on to what states and products are being promoted during the news hours. The audience is in its conditioned state (usually some form of fear-tinged state). The fancy lights, Chyrons and video transitions are in effect. The beautiful but stern and earnest anchors deliver the lines (some might say disingenuously). Cut to advertising – the solution to the public's ills. Read about Chyrons below, then we're on to the solution section.

Broadcast News Technology: What's a Chyron?

A Chyron is sometimes referred to as the "lower third" in the broadcast news business. That's where Chyrons are usually deployed. Chyrons are the graphical and typographical notifications, definitions, summaries, clarifications and general hype that are printed colorfully at the bottom of a newscast. The major networks and cable news networks put them everywhere these days. They've been dutifully lampooned on shows like SNL (see above), where the anchors fight to keep their pretty faces within frame as the Chyrons take over the screen. They're named after the company that originally supplied the graphics to broadcasters.

Who Advertises? (Solutions)

Let's take a specific look at who advertises what and where. Advertising is everywhere, of course. It's on buses, in the sky, on buildings, on the floor of the supermarket, wrapped around cars, on license plate frames, on web pages, in emails, in text messages, on "free" products and services, embedded in games and movies, and prominently featured in TV news broadcasts. It's everywhere – always conditioning us to think about improving our lives or avoiding some feared state of life. It's way out ahead of us and continually hen-pecking our brains.

We're not going to address everything in this section, but we'll start with TV news, because that's a creature that's been around for a while and seems stuck in some distinct patterns. And it fits the theme of this course/text.

So – who are the big advertisers on those nightly slots that seem to never end from 5pm to 11:30pm and beyond on the cable networks? A short list of frequent fliers follows:

- Military
- Politicians
- Orgs/501(c)(3)/non-profit/causes
- Media/entertainment/network promos
- Electronics & mobile phone providers/services
- Automobiles
- Banking/Finance
- Travel services and sites
- Insurance (auto, home, life, retirement)
- Alarms/security
- Pharma and OTC medicines
- Manufacturing
- Food/market
- Household, cleaning and hygiene products
- Diet & exercise products

Let's take a more in depth look at each one of these, looking at the products sold and the motivations behind the advertiser and the potential buyer.

Military: In more naïve times, we wouldn't think of the military as a seller of something. Today, however, anything and everything that has any kind of budget buys advertising in order to move its agenda forward. Ever since disbanding the selective service draft after Vietnam, the military has been forced to encourage or persuade recruits to fill its ranks. Tanks have to be manned, planes need flying, and they need young, fit bodies to fill those positions, learn valuable skills and take some very daunting risks to say the least. Military advertising campaigns glamorize the upsides, encourage young people to pay for school by joining the military, and promise life-long skills, as long as you live through any wars you get into. Military publicity, PR and advertising are also prominent at popular sporting events.

Politicians: In case you hadn't noticed, politics and government pay well. Maybe not for your local city councilman but certainly for those who can afford to advertise on network TV. Everything from candidates and causes to referendums and propositions are advertised on TV, and the results can be downright nauseating. With advertising and public figures (like politicians, celebrities and the like) all bets are off. The First Amendment allows slanderous and libelous speech to be hurled at candidates without fear of legal action. So, you'll see some pretty outrageous advertising around campaign seasons. A lot of that continues into the politician's term, as well, since campaigning has become a year-round sport for many elected officials, especially in the higher ranks like representatives, senators and presidents. This is a fairly recent development (Franklin Roosevelt popularized the concept early on with his "fireside chats" on radio, but in the past 20 years it's become much more intense). Political ads typically exploit the public's worst fears. Sometimes they'll play to high aspirations, but they're usually hit-jobs on their opponents and the policies of their opponents (or the other side of the issue, per a ballot proposition). We have a complete section on how the political election cycle feeds the TV news/broadcast/cable station revenue stream in Part 8. In short, politicians, parties, PACs, and campaigns pay out huge money to the networks and media publishers in 2-year and 4-year election cycles.

Orgs/501(c)(3)/nonprofit/causes: A lot of people place perhaps too much trust into "non-profit" organizations. They are, however, some of the most greed-driven agencies known to the public. As you may have heard, many of the leaders at the helm of the most respected, altruistic organizations take home handsome salaries and enjoy incredible perks. (Case in point – Red Cross CEO Marsha Evans in 2005):

Post-military career [edit]

After retiring from the military, Evans was named executive director of the Girl Scouts of the USA. She held that position from 1998 through 2002. In 2002 she became president and Chief Executive Officer of the American Red Cross. She resigned under pressure in 2005 following a series of disagreements with the organization's board of directors accepting a severance package valued at $780,000 [3]

She was the director of Lehman Brothers until the company declared bankruptcy in 2008.[4]

She was appointed to the board of directors of the LPGA by then-Commissioner Carolyn Bivens in early 2009, after serving on the commissioner's advisory council in 2007 and 2008.[5] In addition to serving on the LPGA board, Evans also serves on the boards of Office Depot, Weight Watchers International, Huntsman and the U.S. Naval Academy Foundation.[6] In 2008, she earned $953,000 in cash and other compensation in exchange for her service on these boards.[7]

Evans also engages in public speaking where her booking fee is between $20,000 and $30,000 per speech.[8]

That's from Wikipedia here: http://bit.ly/2r1WYyC

Media/entertainment/network promos: The networks promote their own shows, of course. This is the promotion that feeds viewers back into the networks other news segments, specials, and entertainment programming. You'll notice this in play during really big events like the Super Bowl. Whatever network is airing the football game will hammer on their new and thriving shows throughout the broadcast. This helps them gather up viewers in a snowball fashion. It's advertising that feeds even more advertising. If you start watching one of the promoted shows, you buy into a whole new realm of messages related to that particular show and its audience. That's smart advertising.

Networks are also required by law to air a certain number of public service ads (crafted by government agencies) during any given day, month or year. More on this later.

Electronics & mobile phone providers/services: Electronics are cool, and we buy them with frenzied delight every year. The promise of electronics is that they'll connect us with friends and family, improve our health (think of all the FitBit and Apple Watch style apps, protect us (911 and amber alerts), entertain us, and generally make our lives one heck of a party. The reality is a little different, though. A lot of us resent our electronics. We consider them a ball and chain – a device that's enslaved us instead of setting us free. Both outlooks are legitimate, and a little of each is true for all of us. Advertisers only give you the promise and the dream, however. They want you to load up on watches, Kindles, Amazon Echos, iPhones, iPads, Surface tablets, stereo equipment, computers, TVs and more.

Automobiles: The single biggest purchase most people ever make – besides a home – will be an automobile. Maybe we'll be driven by self-driving cars someday. Maybe everyone will use Uber only services that are self-driving. But today, the reality is that you're probably going to be driving a car.

Drugs: Let's just call these what they are. A pharmaceutical is just a fancy word for drug but without all the negative associations. Pharma companies are heavily invested in solving health problems via patented drugs. As the saying goes, "for every ill there's a pill." They go to great lengths to cover the negative side effects in their advertising. You can hear all the horrific side effects that they're required to list by law, but they mess with the presentation. This from a 2016 Business Insider article: https://read.bi/2r0vppp

"Some ads use one narrator to talk about the benefits of the drug and a different actor to recite the risks — in a less engaging voice. Or the warning section may be written with more complex sentence structures, to make it harder for viewers to absorb." Over the counter drugs are not so great for us either, though many do serve their purposes during times of relative discomfort. We don't need to debate health policy here, but just know that a lot of money is spent advertising prescription and over the counter (OTC) drugs to the public. Hence – a lot of money is made selling those solutions.

What's Being Sold? FUD-A

You may have heard this acronym before – Fear, Uncertainty and Doubt. It's a state that advertisers prefer to have their audiences in. We'll add a fourth state here that's also useful to advertisers – Aspirational. These are ideal states for a feeling of contrast that can happen to news viewers. You get this barrage of information (the news) about how brutal the world is and how dangerous it is, then they hit you with advertising that solves problems, corrects health, allays fears and offers hope and help to a beleaguered world.

Here are the FUD-A categories and some of the news topics that fit them:

- Fear – personal safety in peril
  - Murders
  - Foreign governments/terrorists
  - Disease
  - Drugs
  - Others/hungry, starving children
  - Diet, medical problems
- Uncertainty/Doubt
  - Health – caffeine vs. decaf, carb vs. low carb, meat vs. no meat
  - Financial markets boom and bust
  - Economy and jobs
  - Computer virus/cyber/security
  - Weather, warming, cooling, storms, chance
- Aspiration
  - Personal appearance
  - Fame and wealth
  - Better mind, body, spirit, location, job

So what kinds of solutions map nicely to these states of discomfort and aspiration? Let's break them into some fun categories.

False Solutions – I'm not claiming that these are all false solutions, however most people do not receive a lot of high-value help from each of these solutions. When the police are at your house, for example, it's usually not a preventative thing. There's a problem that's already happened. You'd be far better off, in terms of health and sanity, to avoid situations that require the police. If your life is similar to what's playing on the 5 O'clock news, you've got some serious re-evaluation to consider. Of course, you've been taught in school that your vote solves everything. . . or at the very least, that it's some pristine, all-powerful virtue signal that's your American birthright. Voting is a good thing. That's true. But it has become somewhat of a cynical ritual these days. On the national stage, we vote in who we want, then the other 49% who didn't want them in engages in legal and highly-productive obstructionism for the duration of the politician's term. This happens to both parties, and it's kind of baked into the bicameral government structure, the courts and the executive branches – checks and balances and all. There are other "solutions." Some organizations that you see advertised on TV want you to consider a donation to their cause as a virtuous vote or virtue signal. You get a sticker to put on your car, or you can change your Twitter icon to signal that you're a conscientious or righteous person. This is a crucial point to remember – you sending money to some cause or .ORG is not a vote. It's more complicated, and you need to evaluate non-profits to see if and how the money you donate is being spent for the purpose you intended. In many cases, it's not. It's merely supporting a complex bureaucracy that's not all that good at solving problems in the real world (sound like something familiar? . . bloated government?). Ok – enough qualifying about what is and isn't a solution. Here's the short list of policy, person and product solutions to all the trouble that's on the news:

Politicians: You have to make up your mind on this one. If you're cynical and perhaps a bit realistic, you realize that you alone are responsible for the path of your life. Yes, there are events and people beyond your control, but the choices you make ultimately shape fate of your existence. There are plenty of self-help and philosophy books out there that agree. Politicians can make a great mess of things and drive everyone crazy (on both the left and right), but your day-to-day life trundles along in a fairly predictable manner, and you really don't have access to any politician that can change things in the short term. They won't get you a raise, pay for your sushi, get your brother or sister to stop bugging you, or fix your broken iPhone screen. I realize that very serious long-term issues are shaped by politicians and voters, but as the news presents things – issues, events and their solutions are an emergency, *right now!* The news presents itself in full-on, hair-on-fire mode every day, every broadcast, every year, *always*. Politicians are the characters they follow along with in this fire drill, but politicians are operating from an entirely different perspective. They want to get on the news and stay in the public eye, because they're interested in getting re-elected. That requires them to appear smart and in tune with the public's interests as often as they can. When the news broadcast breaks for a commercial by a politician (or a one-page ad in a publication), that politician is looking for your vote or money based on some recent emergency that they've stirred up with the news outlets or some long-term strategy that plays out over the course of a 2-year or 4-year election cycle.

Police: As mentioned earlier, you're better off if you don't need your problems solved by law enforcement. Police happenings get some of the most tantalizing, shocking and outrageous coverage in every newscast and newspaper, but they don't serve to solve your problems. That outrageousness only serves to stoke your paranoia about drugs, break-ins, home security, juvenile mischief and so on. There are products you can buy to alleviate some of those fears.

Policy/rules: These are related to politicians and even corporate policies that are influenced by public sentiment stirred up by the news. People are behind the rules, of course (politicians, the CEO, the town crier, etc.). They can get baked into products over the long haul, as well. Aspirin and Ibuprofen bottles never had seals on them, for example. We have news outrage over a poisoning scandal in the 1980's to thank for that (look it up with the keywords Tylenol and cyanide – seven people died). If you have to wait for a rule or a policy change to solve your particular problem, you've got problems.

Initiatives/votes/elections/laws/petitions: You can vote in elections to try to get initiatives passed and politicians into office.

Democracy works well with these mechanisms. Get out the vote efforts are certainly worthy of admiration. This process is all we've got, and it's flawed. But, in the nightly news or daily Facebook news feed reading session where advertising is posited as a solution, it's not going to solve your day-to-day problems. That model just isn't going to work, but it's the one we've all bought into. Watch the news, get outraged, fire up to vote, go home pissed off later, when our guy or issue doesn't get elected. Or get mad at your friends when their guy (who you hate) wins. That's just not a model for emotional health. Ok – end of that tirade. When you sign a petition, it's a little different. You're hoping that the signed petition will get an issue onto a ballot or get some politician recalled (booted out of office, actually). Is it an effective solution to your problems? First off, do you know if the issue even got on the ballot? Think back to a time when you signed a petition at Coachella or outside your local market. Someone clever may have caught your attention and explained their particular issue in a way that got you interested in taking action (like signing their form and maybe changing your Twitter icon). Can you remember the outcome? Did your life change? Was the cause or proposition solved or completed? Doubtful. We're not all the best activists.

Products – face creams, operations, pills, electronics, security systems, etc.: Actual products – which make up the majority of the advertising on a typical nightly news broadcast – might be the most dubious of all the solutions. Here are a few of them that stand out:

http://bit.ly/2HpJGad

VIAGRA
COMMERCIAL
KELLY KING

153

http://bit.ly/2r0xnWP

SAMUEL JACKSON
CAPITAL ONE
COMMERCIAL

http://bit.ly/2Hs1uln

BRINKS HOME SECURITY
COMMERICAL
WRONG DOOR

http://bit.ly/2HqyrhU

AMBIEN
ROOSTER
COMMERCIAL

http://bit.ly/2HpSTzj

JEB BUSH
2016
COMMERCIAL YOUTUBE

Let's think about these one by one. The first is a pill (Viagra) that, you know, well you know. It starts with a very real fear. Some guys have trouble with that particular business. This is an expensive little blue drug that solves the problem. Who knows (or cares!) what the side effects are. The network certainly doesn't. In 2014, big pharma spent $4.54 billion on advertising, with Pfizer, the maker of the drug, leading the way in ad dollars spent. A lot of that cash went to the TV networks.

http://bit.ly/2Hwa02Q

A big chunk of that ad spend – just one year, remember – went toward convincing a very specific demographic (men of a certain age and medical condition) that a little pill could transform their sex lives. That's a huge promise and a highly persuasive proposition. It's the kind of proposition that works with the network TV model. People of that age group (wives, girlfriends and the men themselves) watch the evening news (as well as sports and other entertainment programming), and the message gets across loud and clear, even despite the long list of potential side effects at the end of the ads.

Think about the Capital One ad. What are they selling? A credit card and the potential to buy cool stuff. . . with a twist. They position the solution as a way to make cash! A cash-back card! Woo-hoo! As if you magically use a credit card and make money in the process – the beauty of cash-back rewards.

What they don't tell you is that Capital One has one of the highest APRs (Annual Percentage Rate) of any card out there! That's the interest percentage they charge you when you don't pay the balance in full. You can look into that in finance class. Bottom line: Card holders – not all of them (some people do pay their balances in each billing period) – pay for all that "cash back" and more via exorbitant interest rates of 23% and upwards per annum. Every dollar you don't pay off gets charged 23 cents in interest payments over the year. Woo-hoo! It's a great business model and one worth hiring Samuel Jackson to pitch on network TV.

What fears do they play off of? Not being able to buy cool stuff might be one. Perhaps it's more aspirational. But there's an implicit fear that you might be missing out on lots of cash if you used some other credit card. Jackson claims it's the heavyweight champ of reward programs. It's really just a fake solution that creates more problems for the people who buy into the card. The fact is that not everyone is great with their money, and the interest payments bring in huge revenues for that bank.

How about Brinks Home Security? This one really goes for the fear. And it's kind of dumb. The guy breaks in even though the woman is talking through the door. Maybe he's a deaf robber. The solution (at $100/month) is to have all these sensors and alarms installed at your house to alert you before trouble starts – but it didn't even work that way in the commercial! Bad production. Anyway, the message comes across: Loved ones saved by beeping alarms and a call from a friendly Brinks person.

This particular kind of commercial fits just perfectly into any newscast that's filled with fear, robberies, break-ins, fires, police chases and other criminal mayhem. You get a huge dose of the "real" crazy world out there via the news anchors, then they break for a commercial, and you've got a fool-proof way to protect yourself from the big, bad world out there. The odds of a break-in or a home fire are miniscule, however.

And how about the Ambien commercial? Interesting it's a one minute ad, but the pitch/benefits play out in the first 20 seconds of the ad. The next 40 seconds are all about side effects and dangers! The premise is that if you wake up in the middle of the night, you're affecting your waking health. Simple enough. If you don't get a lot of sleep, you'll be burned out the next day. The solution is a pill. That's the opposite of what we tell the kids. Popping pills to solve physical and mental health problems isn't always the best recipe. There are certainly important uses for pharmaceutical drugs, but you don't just get an Ambien prescription because you woke up in the middle of the night – as this video story portrays. There's no info about whether you should see a psychiatrist, a therapist or any of that. As a story it's just simple and quick. Can't sleep, pop the Ambien. That ad played incessantly on TV shows over the years, too. We've all seen or heard it in the background, unconsciously, consciously or subliminally. They beat these thoughts into your heads so it doesn't seem like that big of a deal when and if you come across the sleeplessness problem.

The final ad is a political ad for Jeb Bush during the 2016 Republican presidential primaries. It's a different animal and very long at three minutes and thirteen seconds. It's a problem/solution case study format, with multiple stories. The topics range from abuse and disability health to jobs and education. Jeb Bush's solutions are then explained once that plays out, as if people couldn't pick themselves up without the help of a politician. There might be some truth to that, but the claims for responsibility probably lie with several personal, family, community, municipality and state players (which may include Bush). It's kind of insulting when the worker guy says Bush allowed companies like his to grow. There may have been some tax advantages in the state of Florida favorable to that particular company, but it's a bit of a stretch. You can check out the other stories in the video. The music is emotional and uplifting toward the end. It's done well, as in the movies.

Exercise: Take a look at an evening newscast and try to make some sense of the structure. What kinds of stories lead the newscast? Politics? Events? Tragedy? Issues? What advertisements follow that "A-Block?" What kinds of stories take up the middle portion of the newscast? What ads follow that "B-Block?" What kinds of stories make up the final "C-Block?" What advertising follows? Chart this activity for a week then we'll convene on Monday to discuss your findings. By the way, A, B and C blocks are TV and radio industry terms that describe segments of a broadcast. You could have D, E, F, etc. blocks, as well. An hour-long local news broadcast typically has four blocks, with A containing news, B more news, C sports, and D with human interest or more casual or uplifting stories.

Why Live TV Events Are Better for Ad Buys

Live TV events, like breaking news and sports events that are best viewed as they're happening, have ads that are more likely to reach audiences. When you have the TV on, and you're not manning the DVR pause button, you're bound to get hit with some ads. Some people mute the TV and some pause the DVR, but many keep it on as things are developing and get stuck consuming some ads as the breaks come.

For the advertiser, this is a valuable situation, because their messages get through, and people are more likely to buy the products (some day – remember – many products have imprinted their brand on your brain and don't influence purchase until years or even decades later). Remember our earlier discussion about advertising influence, as well. Most people think they're impervious to advertising, but it's simply not true. TV advertising revenue (as an industry) was nearly $71 billion in 2016 (Statista.com).

http://bit.ly/2HsBczl

That money is not spent in vain. Advertising in all its forms works, and if you recognize this you have an advantage over others when you're analyzing campaigns directed at you. It's not a sin to buy products, but you can be wise about your consumption and not fall prey to impulse buys and nonsense products.

Live TV is also one of the key reasons people continue buying cable TV, by the way. With Netflix, Amazon Prime, HBO Go and the like, many viewers – called "cord cutters" – ditch cable all together. If they don't care about live news broadcasts and like getting that info via Twitter or whatever other online channel, they can certainly cut that cord. Same goes for people who just don't care about live sports. HD sports fans, however, are out of luck. They need to keep paying for 512 channels just to watch five or six of them! This may change as cable subscription rates decline.

Man on the Street Interviews

If you've seen network late night comedy shows (Kimmel, Fallon, Colbert, etc.), you've seen 'man of the street' interviews. They're used in straight or hard news, as well. The station or comedy show uses the man on the street to put whatever information or message they want into the story. They pick and choose the message that fits their story, and that becomes the truth. It's edited in, and a done deal. The viewer is then presented with a news product that:

1. Is biased by the reporter/editor/producer
2. Is just errant or uninformative because the reporter was lazy
3. Some combination of the above

With comedy, it works great, because the interview team can gather up dozens of reasonable answers to the question but then only use the really stupid answers as a representation of the entire public.

Here's a funny one about gluten from the Jimmy Kimmel show:

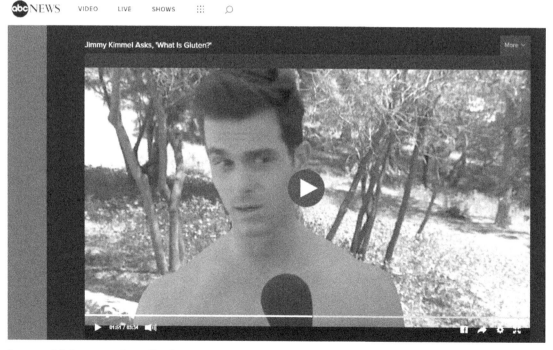

https://abcn.ws/2r2fhnk

Do Today's Ads Influence Next Year *Or Next Decade* Purchases?

Many of the things we buy are purchased months and sometimes years after we've seen an ad. This is particularly effective with things like insurance, which requires brand knowledge and trust, and beer, which hit kids in ads at an early age but catches up to them later when they're of drinking age (or close) and are making lifestyle choices about what kinds of alcohol to associate themselves with. The same goes for automobiles. As a youth, you identify with lifestyles and promises that are associated with cars, then that information influences you at a much later time, when you're able to drive and can afford to buy a car on your own.

These ads often feature celebrities. Audi uses Ricky Gervais, Lincoln hired Matthew McConaughey,

Ricky Gervais – Audi: http://bit.ly/2qZKY0G

DUES
GERVAIS
AUDI

Jean Claude Van Damme – Volvo: http://bit.ly/2r0QeRG

VAN DAMME
VOLVO
TRUCKS

If you look at all these ads, you'll catch on to a theme. Focus groups and deep data analysis must have turned up this particular approach to car buyers. It's especially prominent with the Audi and Volvo ads. By the time you're grown up and are looking for a car, you've had your fair share of hard knocks. You're hardened and battle tested. The Audi ad does it cleverly with Queen lyrics from *We are the Champions*. They're very aspirational, but they both offer this idea that you have to pass some tests to get to these cars. Your experience, moxie, scars, mistakes and travails lead you to these payoffs.

Both of those ads use high-profile celebrities that may have made impressions on viewers during their younger years.

Kate Upton – Mercedes: http://bit.ly/2qZLpbk

UPTON 2013
MERCEDES
SUPER BOWL

This Mercedes ad ups the ante a bit. It includes performer Usher, actor Willem Dafoe, and model Kate Upton. The promise of sex, fame and race car driver status are the clever motivators. All that, however, doesn't have to be part of the deal. It could be perceived as negative, in fact. But the imagery does the job. The ad plays to those aspirations while also touching on reason. The guy who's offered a deal with the devil (Dafoe) can get all that good stuff or something close for just $30K by the end of the advertisement.

Celebrities work well in these ads, because:

1. They're already good actors so the director has an easy time of it
2. They come pre-loaded with perceptions (Dafoe works great as someone evil, and Upton oozes sex)
3. Their personal value as someone successful (Usher) associates that value with the brand and the car buyer's aspirations
4. They're appealing to the eye – most actors just have to be this way, even if they have a tinge of ugly to them

Most people are entertained by this kind of advertising, but many are somewhat naïve when it comes to their power. Ask any of your friends if they think they're persuaded to make purchasing decisions based on TV ads, and you'll probably get a snarky response. To a man, people think they're immune to ads.

On the surface, it makes sense. We see tons of advertising, and we don't consciously connect our purchase decisions back to the ads that have soaked into our brains over the decades. It's interesting, however, what we learn and remember from ads. You could ask those same friends what their perception of a particular beer, car or insurance company is, and they'll usually give you a response that's right in line with the intended perceptions that the company's ads convey. Ask them about Jameson whiskey and if they'd drink it. Ask them to associate a word with Mercedes, Subaru, Toyota, Jeep or Range Rover. Ask them to tell you what they think about Jack in The Box, Outback Steak or Wing Stop.

Here are my responses to the whiskey, cars and restaurants:

- Jameson – man's drink, quality, classy, Irish roots, Irish pride
- Mercedes – wealth, real estate professionals, quality, German obsession
- Subaru – hippy conscientious, outdoors, humble, adventurous, democrat
- Toyota – practical, value, trusted, durable, long life/mileage (This last bit is a holdover from Toyota ads that featured odometer readings in the 1970's and 1980's –

the people in the ads showed you their 250,000 and 300,000+ mile odometers and then jumped into the air – "oh what a feeling, Toyota!" How's that for recall!)

- Jeep – adventure, outdoors, mud on fenders, off-road, military, utility
- Range Rover – wealth, exclusivity, elite, solid, all-wheel drive on mountains and off-roading
- Jack in the Box – munchies, late night eats, hangover food, grease, vice, dark side
- Outback Steak – Australia, modest budget eats, consistent across the country, bloomin' onion, beer and full bar service
- Wing Stop – Sports, NFL, day with the boys, TVs, gambling, grease, vice, bar food treat

Advertising works – even on me.

You can extend this friend asking experiment even further. Ask them if they think other people are influenced by ads, and they'll probably say yes. Think about it. Would Mercedes spend $5 million on a Super Bowl ad if they didn't *know* that it drives sales?

Three Kinds of Advertising Timing

TV ads can be divided into many different style, approach and influence categories. However, there are several timing patterns that are important to recognize. As in the discussion in the previous section, some ads influence you to buy the product years later – like with insurance, automobiles and beer. Other ads influence you to buy right away. These are the "act now!" style ads where the product looks very enticing, solves a real problem, and creates a sense of urgency. These are things like the Sham-Wow, the Pocket Hose, and ProActiv acne treatments. They often have offer timers that put time limits on the promotion and feature web sites where the product can be ordered from a tablet, laptop or phone.

Option 5 - Watching Function

25.00 NIS

QUANTITY

Lithograph - Height: 9" x W ▾   1   **Add to Cart**

● 566 watching   40 sold in the last hour

250 of 400 sold

00	04	52	47
Days(S)	Hours	Minutes	Seconds

Sale Ends Once The Timer Hits Zero!

Notice in the image above that the shopping cart also includes how many people are watching the item, how many were sold out of a total available, and how many sold in the last hour. These are often referred to as "nudges." One is social proof – everyone watches this or wants it. The limitation on availability introduces scarcity. The time for the deal ads more scarcity and urgency. It's all designed to motivate and persuade you. Some of the web tools that allow the cart to show these numbers are connected directly to inventory and sales systems, so they're legit. Most tools for building these kinds of shopping cart pages, however, allow the vendor to fudge the numbers and create false scarcity. Gasp!

There's a third kind of timing for ads, as well. This is for purchases that usually happen at the supermarket or online at sites like Amazon. The brand and the product become impressed upon the viewer so they can easily recall the item on their next shopping spree. These are ads usually associated with the big consumer packaged goods (CPG) companies like Unilever and Proctor & Gamble. Examples include Tide, Vaseline, Lipton, Ben & Jerry's, Bounty, Charmin, Crest, Dawn. People develop shopping habits around these brands and buy them whenever they're in a market. The CPG companies want to develop life-long habits with their customers, and their subtle ad campaigns cultivate this through the years.

Tamiflu: An Ad Buy Case Study

For this advertising case study we're going to look at a popular prescription drug that's used to lessen the effects of influenza – Tamiflu (oseltamivir). We'll show a couple of videos so you can hear two different reports, a week apart, that have completely different information about the drug and its effects. The reports are not taking on the same circumstances or stories related to the drug, but there's a distinct difference between the two. If you're reading along and are not near a computer/phone/tablet, check the summary box to the right to get the gist of the reporting.

Here's the report that aired on a local Dallas, Texas CBS station on January 18, 2018:

https://cbsloc.al/2r5dXAv

January 18 Report Summary: The story reports on a rare side effect that occurs in children who take Tamiflu. One example they give is an earlier report from a family whose 6-year-old daughter tried to jump out of a second story window after taking the drug. Another story, the report continues, is about a teenage girl from Indianapolis, Indiana who got the flu, took Tamiflu and then started "hallucinating bugs on her body and the devil's voice in her ear." The dad wonders if his daughter is possessed (pretty strong feeling and emotion here). She was hospitalized for 2 months, had a feeding tube, and "was incoherent, unable to move her hands and feet for several weeks." A year later she still has problems. Stories like these run every year, and they're serious. People do have these reactions, but not all of them with the flu are taking Tamiflu. Sometimes kids that have the flu and are not taking the drug have similar symptoms. There is emerging evidence that a nasal spray flu "shot" when combined with Tamiflu is the problem. The combination may cause these symptoms.

Eight days later, the ABC national nightly news aired this report:

https://abcn.ws/2r2zrxF

January 26, 2018 Report Summary: The report starts with some background about a woman who died three days after contracting the flu. The stage is set, and we have a very scary, true story from which to jump off and discuss the matter further. Next, the report says the Centers for Disease Control (CDC) recommends that some people take Tamiflu as a prophylactic or flu preventative.

By the way, the drug is commonly taken to lessen the effects of the flu *after* it's contracted, not before. The story goes on to detail more deaths of children from the flu. Then there's info about how older people are being admitted to the hospital for the flue, and how that's the reverse of what's usual. Typically young people go to the hospital for the flu, and old people not as much. So they're now including two big demographics in the story.

Then the anchor in the studio has a visiting doctor next to him (we really don't know much about her), and he asks the doctor (and I'm paraphrasing), *so this year seniors, children and the baby boomers and caretakers (huge demo), should they be taking Tamiflu, as well?*

The anchor tees up the doctor by talking about how her daughter is home with the flu with much empathy. He then remarks about how she, the doctor, was on Tamiflu and how she can easily get the drug because she's a doctor. She agrees with that and then launches into a pitch about how vulnerable, high-risks groups should take Tamiflu as a prophylactic measure. These include pregnant women, those over age 65, "anyone with a chronic medical condition like asthma," or anyone with a weakened immune system. Then the anchor talks about how we used to think that people should take Tamiflu within 48 hours of symptoms of the flu and asks the doctor if there's new information about that old info. She says that's the "old thinking" and now new data suggest that it's now useful to take Tamiflu even after that 48 hour window.

This report shows up on several ABC shows throughout the week, with different formats and anchors.

So this is what we're dealing with:

The lead in is a fear piece about someone who developed the flu and died. Then, at the 1:04 mark, the gears switch, and they start talking about CDC recommendations regarding Tamiflu, which is made by Hoffmann-La Roche Inc. and Gilead Sciences, Inc.

If you've ever seen news reporting on the flu, you've probably noticed that the reports include information about getting the flu shot. Many urge the public to get one in very strong terms. What's weird about this report is that in the entire report they never mention the flu shot. And, the alternative to Tamiflu, Relenza (zanamivir), which is made by a competitive company in Australia but licensed in the U.S. by GlaxoSmithKline, is a big competitor of Hoffmann-La Roche.

If you follow that video along, it begins to sound as if the doctor and the anchor are in cahoots, promoting the solution to the flu in the same breath. The questions are coordinated even to the point of almost sounding rehearsed. The fear segments lead into the guest doctor who promotes it. The anchor almost cheerleads. They go on and on. Should loved ones with the flu take Tamiflu? According to the doc, almost everyone should – the pregnant, old, and weak. Take it after the 48 hour window. Yes! That's "old thinking!" No that shouldn't be a reason to *withhold* treatment. As if not using Tamiflu is somehow a withholding of something splendid. Contrast that thinking with the prior report eight days earlier.

So what are we to deduce? Was this a pure media buy mixed in with some old anecdotal stories about flu and deaths? It definitely wasn't a general report on flu dos and don'ts that includes multiple suggestions (Tamiflu, Relenza and flu shot). That would be balanced, fair and complete coverage. This one was all Tamiflu to the exclusion of everything else. Pretty transparent, huh?

Think back to the earlier report. *Your kids might become possessed!* Did the doctor on the second report miss that other information?!?! This one says to take it even if you don't have the flu! Take it to prevent the flu!

Ok – off of the soap box for a sec. Yes, there are side effects to Tamiflu like there are side effects to the flu shot, but the earlier report seems to scare up fears that are totally ignored in the second report. Granted, these are two different networks and different sources for each story, but what is the public supposed to think?

It reminds me of the caffeine/no caffeine, coffee is good for you, it's bad for you debates that have gone on for years. Is this the way a news station or network pulls more money out of advertisers? Coffee producers used to be some of the biggest advertisers on TV. I'm not sure how prevalent they are now. But it's a great concept that we may never totally understand, unless we work in an advertising agency that's buying ads for these stations (or at the company which is purchasing the ads). Did the company that makes Tamiflu eventually get peeved or frustrated with the negative reporting that surrounds their product every flu season? Did they cave into network pressure and buy the ad in order to counter the negative claims? Even more conspiratorially, do network news programs run negative stories about companies they want to advertise on their networks. That's a sinister take on it, but anything's possible.

What is a "Squeeze Page?"

In the old days, people that wanted to sell things without advertising on the radio, TV or in major magazines or newspapers used something called direct mail to pitch their solutions (it still exists, of course). These were initially formatted as business letters, but they evolved into a format that you might recognize as the classic internet squeeze page. Other direct pitches also occur via plain old email, too.

The company selling anything from stock picking services to exercise equipment would buy a list of names and addresses from a list broker then send out the same letter, packet or other unique marketing piece directly to their potential prospects. List brokers got good at slicing and dicing their lists so they could develop custom audiences to pitch and sell to companies looking to send out direct mail. If you wanted people who fish, the list company might triangulate a list of people that subscribe to *Field & Stream* magazine and sell that list to you.

Here's an old direct mail piece encouraging women to buy panty hose:

**Do your Panty Hose
make you feel pretty?
Do they fit perfectly
and wear and wear?**

Hello,

I'm Sarah Smith, and want to share something my husband said the other day that just about sums up the reasons why you may be disappointed with most panty-hose made today. Eddie said:

"Most other panty-hose come in two or three sizes today but some of the prettiest and most shapely legs don't!"

This is so true. He couldn't be more right!

Most of us switched to panty-hose a few years ago and then what happened?

The manufacturers started switching sizes on us-- now some make only one size and expect the woman who buys them to jump for joy and think she will get a comfortable fit and look like a fashion model.

Honestly, I just don't know how most women put up with the hit-or-miss fit, poor quality and dime store appearance they get when they buy panty-hose today.

Even the 99¢ "Grocery Store" type is too much to pay for something that doesn't make you look and feel good!

I love panty-hose and hope they are here to stay- but they certainly should be made to fit properly and give

This first page sets up the problem nicely, with a personal anecdote that audiences for this type of piece care about – husbands.

Eight into three won't go!

you stylish good looks--and last a while--and if we pay quality prices, we should get quality hosiery.

Eddie started selling quality hosiery by mail, by the dozen, over 30 years ago. Now he has over 500,000 satisfied customers--many who have been regular customers for over 30 years. So--

If you are fed up with baggy, ill-fitting hose--

If you find you can't get the same size twice--

If the quality is poor or inconsistent--

If you'd like to try something better, something that is different and really worth the money you pay--

I'd like to invite you to try our National brand. See for yourself what a pleasure it is to have panty-hose that fit like a smooth second skin--but don't come apart or fade after the second wearing.

I just wish you could see all the nice letters we get from women of all ages who write to tell us how much

The transition from the first page to the next sets up the dream scenario in the beginning. The reveal up top is that her husband is involved in some sort of direct mail panty hose solutions the previously mentioned issues. Then comes the pitch and the benefits.

trouble they have had with store bought panty-hose that don't fit -- and how they love their new found National Panty-Hose.

They tell us how nice it is to have sheer panty-hose at last, that have crotch pieces and panels--and are made of the most expensive materials. They say our panty-hose give them the beauty, the comfort, long wear, and confidence they have needed for years.

Over and over again, they say in so many, many ways --

8 into 3 just won't go!

When you try to make 8 sizes of women fit into only 3 sizes of panty-hose--nobody gets a good fit. If you are short they sag and if you are tall they pull down. If you are slim they bag and if your figure is full they bind. Even someone in the middle doesn't get a good fit because the panty-hose were designed to fit everybody--which means we all end up with ill-fitting panty-hose that does nothing for our figures or morale.

That's why Eddie insists on only the finest quality made in eight sizes -- Yes EIGHT separate sizes. When you come to National for your panty-hose -- you are abso-lutely sure of getting a perfect fit. You'll look great, feel

There are some "staged" testimonials, talking points from supposed women who write them about the panty hose all the time. . . followed by a nice little rhyming ditty. Then, more quality, fit and selection features.

good and will be well dressed and attractive. Take your choice from four regular sizes and four queen sizes.

You don't ever need to worry when you order from National. Our money-back guarantee protects you completely. If you should ever get a pair that is not perfect in every way -- Eddie just doesn't argue. He simply sends you another pair -- no questions asked. (I've seen him send a whole dozen, just to be sure the customer was repaid for her trouble and for calling an error to his attention.)

When our customers from out-of-state stop by to say "hello" and pick up a few boxes of hosiery, Eddie always likes to give them something free -- kind of like the free gifts offered on the coupon enclosed.

Your free pair coupon will do more than just bring you some nice free gifts -- buying the National way will bring you freedom -- freedom from being forced to take something less than you deserve -- freedom to choose exactly what you want from National's complete line - 30 styles of panty-hose and stockings.

So if you would like to test wear hosiery that's "tailor made" for YOU -- not for everybody and anybody--

Why not try the National way for yourself. You'll be so glad you did. Why not get a trial order in the mail today. Then you'll see why more than 500,000 women buy with confidence from National.

Sincerely,

Sarah Smith

Sarah Smith

P.S. Remember we ship all orders within 24 hours, too!

NATIONAL *Wholesale Co* INC.
HOSIERY DIVISION

Lexington, North Carolina 27292
(704) 246-5904

A guarantee is classic direct mail and classic salesmanship in print. Free gifts and coupons sweeten the deal. A rousing pitch for freedom and some larger aspiration. Social proof claims that 500,000 women are sharing the customer's buying journey. The clever post script could be right out of modern eBay listing that promises same-day shipping. It's all classic direct response copywriting.

Here's a squeeze page from more current times. This is all one page and all one scroll when you see it on the web, but we'll break it down here and fit it onto text pages as pieces of the whole.

The lead starts with big, bold benefits and promises. Then right into claimed social proof. The video is a nice updated touch, with a pitch from the pitchman himself. Icons highlight benefits, and then more aspirational benefits are in order.

> **Social Proof:** (also known as informational social influence) is a psychological and social phenomenon where people assume the actions of others in an attempt to reflect correct behavior in a given situation. ... This is contrasted with normative social influence wherein a person conforms to be liked or accepted by others.

This next one is more modern and comes from the web (next page):

The pitch starts with a promise and guarantee about avoiding the discomfort and distractions that glasses-wearers confront every day. The main benefits related to unique custom fit glasses then follows.

ANISSA

A custom-fit that's here to stay

Like many people, Anissa has a hard time finding stock eyewear that fits her. Her Topology frames have been distinctly sculpted to her nose bridge and elevate her glasses away from her cheeks, positioning them comfortably on her face and perfectly in front of her eyes.

ALEXIS

The perfect fix for a broken nose

Alexis's nose was on the losing side of a Rugby match. It was broken along his nasal bridge and healed with a slightly crooked shape. His Topology frames have been sculpted asymmetrically, so they perfectly conform to his face.

RITIKA

A solid answer for a shifty situation

Ritika wanted eyeglasses that stay perfectly in place, no matter what the activity. Her Topology frames have been precision-fit to perfectly align her lenses to her field of vision and comfortably sized to never shift or slide down.

Next come testimonial-style case studies, which trumpet the specific benefits of these glasses. The idea is to present real people and their real stories that buttress the brand's promise.

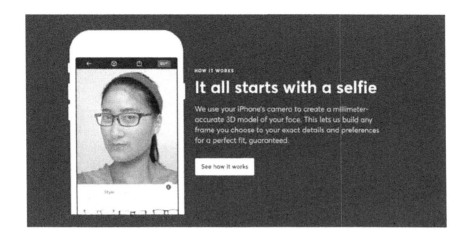

It all starts with a selfie

We use your iPhone's camera to create a millimeter-accurate 3D model of your face. This lets us build any frame you choose to your exact details and preferences for a perfect fit, guaranteed.

See how it works

STYLES

Every frame is a blank canvas

Choosing a style for your glasses is just the beginning. Select your materials, mix and match colors, then adjust the width and size of your frames to create your signature look.

Next, they get into some process and how it works.

Precision-made for any prescription

Our lenses are just as unique as the frames you design. Made-to-order based on your 3D data and frame style, all lenses come with scratch-resistant and anti-reflective coating and can support any prescription, including progressive.

Learn about our lenses

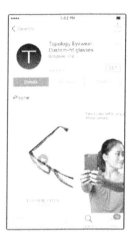

Your signature-fit is just a selfie away

Download the Topology Eyewear app for iPhone and style your perfect eyeglasses or sunglasses today.

Finally, more features, advantages and benefits followed by a call to action - download the app to get started. It's a simple flow that solves a somewhat complex issue for people who wear glasses.

Squeeze pages haven't really changed much over the years.

Here's the general long-form structure for squeeze pages:

- Compelling issue, problem or aspiration
- Explanation of something "insider" or unique that the company learned about that particular problem
- A story about how they came across the ultimate answer (this could also be teased out a bit more by describing multiple failures at coming up with the "eureka" moment)
- A description of the solution and its benefits to the recipient of the communication
- Testimonials from people (often with their photos) who confirm the benefits of the solution
- A pitch to get in on the solution
- A harder pitch
- A reiteration of previously mentioned advantages and benefits
- Yet another pitch
- P.S. exit
- Perhaps another entreaty to take some kind of half-measure
- P.P.S exit
- One last ditch effort at pitching something minor for the recipient to say yes to

Once you get a sense for these formats, you'll start seeing them all over the web. When they're done right, they work. You may have even fallen victim to an over-hyped product or product story via a well-written squeeze page. Some companies lead their email capture sequences with squeeze pages whose only aim is to get your email address. They follow this up with additional messages that sequentially move you closer to the sale. In the marketing business, we call this getting the small yes. 1) Get them to say yes to inputting their Gmail address, 2) Get them to say yes to a video click, 3) Get them to say yes to a webinar, 4) Get them to say yes to a sample download, 5) Get them to say yes to the low-end, economy product, 6) Get them to say yes to the upgraded product and subscription plan. That's a classic drip marketing sequence.

Exercise: Be honest. Go deep into your recent memory and think about something you bought on the web. Did you purchase it immediately? Did you sign up for an email? Did you purchase after reading a whole lot of marketing copy that was dripped out over the course of a little web surfing session or an email sequence? Write down some of the motivations for your purchase, bring them to class, and we'll go over a few of the good ones. You can be anonymous, if you like.

The Business Case Study

What is a case study and how does it relate to psychological persuasion?

In the world of business, companies use customer or client case studies to demonstrate their value to potential customers or prospects.

It's pretty simple, and the format is borrowed from a simpler Greek drama format.

You set up a challenge or an issue that needs to be resolved. Next, you describe the conundrum and the tension involved in solving that particular problem. Then you explain a decision-making process. Finally, you detail how the problem was solved and the emotional, financial, efficiency and cost savings results that were realized.

Simple as that. It's a classic narrative that allows businesses to showcase their solutions within a time-tested format.

Case studies are business gold, because they get customers to go on the record about how they solved their specific issue with the company's product/solution/service.

This is the same format that pops up in advertisements, brochures, squeeze pages, video testimonials . . . and yes movie plots.

Doritos: A Brilliant Native Ad and PR Play

This is a good one, buckle your seatbelts. Once you start looking for these, you'll see them every week if you have any exposure to TV.

Here's the set-up. Doritos released information to the media that they were working on a chip that wouldn't crunch loudly and be messy. The idea? A chip that women could eat without feeling self-conscious or impolite! This wasn't just a whim. The whole thing was set up by their PR firm or advertising agency, and they pretended the female CEO of PepsiCo (the Doritos parent company) came up with the idea.

Here's the brilliant part. The mainstream media went nuts for the story. Some were actually outraged. They brought bags of chips onto the sets of their TV broadcasts and delivered both funny and serious rants against the idea. CNN chimed in, saying it was a bad idea. As if CNN doesn't recognize a publicity stunt when it sees one! NBC's Today Show pooh-poohed the idea. Late night talk show host Seth Meyers had the best zinger, saying, ". . . because there's no more appropriate snack for the #metoo era than a chip that tells women to be quiet?"

Fox News' Greg Gutfeld captured the clips in his humorous but serious take on the subject that includes some real outrage that should have happened over the Iranian crackdown on women protesting wearing head scarves. But, he really just fell for the stunt just like all the others. In fact, he dedicated 6 minutes and 20 seconds to his segment. Check out the part at the 2:30 mark where the panelist with the blonde hair talks about how the company quickly said "just kidding" about the proposal to make the chips. That's a tell. The panelist goes on to lampoon the CEO of the company, as if the CEO is so naïve to consider this in the first place. They were never planning on making the chip.

This is post-Super Bowl advertising brilliance. They're cashing in on a lot of snacking good will from the football event the week before and simply doubling down on all the imprinting they did during the Super Bowl commercials. They got a big bump in popularity and the impressions they make on our minds with all this free advertising.

Here's the clip: http://bit.ly/2qZGBmw

Now, let's play devil's advocate for a bit and take the position of PepsiCo. Let's say this was real news. The CEO thought of this idea, and they were testing it by leaking the information to the press. Maybe that's plausible. Maybe there's a future for gender-specific foods. In some ways there are already products – like Special K and certain dainty yoghurts – that seem to target female audiences in their advertising more than men. Anyway, if they get feedback from news shows and funny anchors about whether this is a good idea . . does that help their case? Don't they already have focus groups in place to test these theories? You don't simply have the CEO leak information then take the temperature of talk show hosts.

So, no, I don't think this was a legitimate floating of an idea to see if it might be favorably received by the press. This was an overt PR stunt – brilliant, by the way – aimed at gathering up as much news coverage as possible without spending a dime. Granted, all the stations with hosts debating this new chip have advertised PepsiCo products and Doritos every day for the past who knows how many decades.

These days, you'll see a lot of this starting on Twitter. The company, PR firm, Ad agency or the brand's spokesperson or spokesmodel ⯑ will Tweet out some provocative message in hopes of virality. This is common practice for A/B testing product ideas or promotion ideas. Authors of books even do it to see which title ideas are playing favorably on social media. Author Tim Ferris of *Four Hour Work Week* fame used that very technique back in 2008 to decide the title of his book. Does Twitterverse like title A or title B? All you have to do is track retweets and likes in a big enough population sample, and you can pick a winner. You can also multivariate test, which is the same concept as A/B, but you just add in more variables to the choice – A, B, C, D, etc.

This was a classic native ad campaign. Convenient that sex and gender played into the fall-out. It's especially delicious for the times we live in and was easy fodder for late night comedy TV shows, newscasts, tweets by famous people etc.

AdAge sums it up nicely (sounds like a promo with the quotes they use in the story!) http://bit.ly/2r3T3BM

Epic: "The reporting on a specific Doritos product for female consumers is inaccurate," a spokeswoman stated in an emailed Monday

evening. "We already have Doritos for women–they're called Doritos, and they're enjoyed by millions of people every day. At the same time, we know needs and preferences continue to evolve and we're always looking for new ways to engage and delight our consumers."

Uber-epic: "When you eat out of a flex bag—one of our single-serve bags—especially as you watch a lot of the young guys eat the chips, they love their Doritos, and they lick their fingers with great glee, and when they reach the bottom of the bag they pour the little broken pieces into their mouth because they don't want to lose that taste of the flavor, and the broken chips in the bottom," <u>she said in the interview, according to a transcript.</u> "Women would love to do the same, but they don't. They don't like to crunch too loudly in public. And they don't lick their fingers generously and they don't like to pour the little broken pieces and the flavor into their mouth."

Advertiser Motivations and Fears

Hypercharged political, social and cultural climates, e.g. the current United States environment, present unique challenges to advertisers. They need to sell products and advertise in order to do so, but they're selling into highly divided and fragmented populations that use equally fragmented media outlets.

You may have transgender people watching MSNBC while country folk are watching Fox News. . . and vice versa. You may have gun rights people watching CNN while some anti-Trumpers are following along on both the Wall Street Journal and Politico. There's a huge mix of overlap and conflicting alignment out there. A lot of people don't even know where they're getting the news. They click on a YouTube video or follow a link from

> **Masthead Defined:** the title of a newspaper or magazine at the head of the front or editorial page.

Facebook, and they don't know who originated the content. Or worse, they don't care or bother to look at the masthead (there must be a newer term for this).

The advertisers are aware of this, and it's very difficult for them to navigate the waters, especially when big national, controversial events go down.

Here are just a few examples of such incidents from AdAge's June 2017 article *The CMO's Guide to Ad Boycotts*:

- "JPMorgan Chase and some local advertisers dropped out of an episode of Megyn Kelly's NBC newsmagazine over an interview with InfoWars founder Alex Jones, who claims the Sandy Hook massacre was a hoax."
- "Delta Air Lines and Bank of America canceled their support for a staging of "Julius Caesar" by New York's Public Theater because the title character, who is murdered, resembled President Trump."
- "JPMorgan Chase revamped its whole ad-tech strategy after its ads landed on a site called Hillary 4 Prison."
- ". . . marketers pulled out of YouTube when reporters found ads served near hate speech and extremist content."

http://bit.ly/2r5gZET

191

The article said: "Promising to protect marketers is the selling tactic of the day." "After yesterday's meetings," said one marketing executive during last week's Cannes ad festival, "I've decided 'brand safety' is the new 'gluten free.'"

Generally speaking, advertisers do not want to run their ads on any media or content outlets (online or off) that are controversial or dubious in nature.

But there are inherent traps involved here. Advertising is a creative endeavor, and when you police everything you lose attention (the main goal of advertising outside of actual purchase conversions).

The AdAge article explains: "What's more, safe content doesn't always help you get noticed. "The temptation is to make things that are unobjectionable and put them in places that are unobjectionable because no one wants to be the next negative or story," MullenLowe's Paul said. "But unobjectionable is invisible, and when brands are fighting for attention, safe is risky.""

Ha! How's that for a Catch 22?!?!

And here's the kicker: "While consumers may say they're going to stop buying your products if you keep advertising in this show or that, King said there's little evidence that they actually follow through. Many weren't buying the given brand in the first place. . ."

Newsjacking Case Study: Dick's Sporting Goods

As you may recall, newsjacking is the practice of hijacking news headlines in order to further a PR campaign or expose a commercial brand. That commercial brand could even be a celebrity or a personality brand like Oprah or Gary Vaynerchuk. Big brands and celebrities are positioned particularly well to grab headlines when they attach themselves to a cause or incident in order to gain exposure or facilitate some type of action on the part of the public.

Dick's Sporting Goods used the practice in early 2018 in a dubious fashion. The retailer announced that they'd be discontinuing sales of AR-15 rifles after February's school shooting in Florida. Sounds like a worthy cause, right? Take the guns off the shelves to eliminate the possibility that someone might come in, buy one and then shoot up a school.

Except, there's a little white lie involved.

Dick's Sporting Goods stores don't carry AR-15s. The chain's 600+ stores across the United States stopped selling AR-15s in 2012. That was six years ago. Technically, the parent company owns Field and Stream stores, of which there are 35 retail locations. Those stores sell AR-15s. But Dick's presented itself in news headlines as some sort of savior by indicating that *Dick's* was taking AR-15s off of the shelves. Kind of shifty, if you ask me.

The big brand, which everyone knows across the country, benefited from a positive boost in the news cycle. They brought attention to both their altruism and their stores. It was free advertising. Almost every news media outlet covered the story in a positive light. There were very few publications that cast some doubt and shame on the brand. Here's one from *The Washington Examiner*.

https://washex.am/2r0EzCv

They called it "just a stunt," which is what it was.

In a way, you could consider it free advertising at the expense of 17 school kids in Florida. Well, not really. But, the company took advantage of a tragedy to further its business interests. They should be boycotted for that alone.

Here's a thought: Wouldn't it be nice to know where the shooter at the

Florida school bought his AR-15? (According to USA Today, it was purchased at a place called Sunrise Tactical Supply.) And why wasn't that splashed all over the headlines and the evening news? What if Dick's Sporting Goods had sold the rifle to the

kid? Would the news have suppressed that information for fear that Dick's might no longer

Fun meme that surfaced just after Dick's stunt.

advertise? Ammunition for thought.

ASIDE: We found that Washington Examiner article by searching Google for the phrase "dick's sporting goods doesn't sell ar-15." Here's a little peek at the SERP (Search Engine Result Page).

All   News   Shopping   Images   Videos   More   Settings   Tools

About 3,840,000 results (0.70 seconds)

Top stories

Walmart, Dick's Sporting Goods Sued by 20-Year-Old Over New Gun Restrictions	Walmart, Dick's Sporting Goods sued by 20-year old over gun policies	20-year-old Oregon man sues Dick's Sporting Goods, Walmart over rifle sale
Newsweek	USA TODAY	CBS News
7 hours ago	10 hours ago	11 hours ago

→ More for dick's sporting goods doesn't sell ar-15

Dick's Sporting Goods took a stand against guns. But will it matter ...
https://www.nbcnews.com/.../dick-s-sporting-goods-took-stand-against-guns-will-it-n8... ▾
5 days ago - The announcement by Dick's Sporting Goods on Wednesday that it would stop selling military-style rifles like the AR-15 was instantly powerful, dominating the news cycle while adding fuel to a gun control debate that has raged since the Feb. 14 shooting at Marjory Stoneman Douglas High School in ...

The first four results (including the "top stories") show how Dick's was sued (this was a new development – the results looked different prior to this lawsuit) and how they "took a stand against guns."

Dick's Sporting Goods' 'new' policy of not selling AR-15 rifles is just a ...
www.washingtonexaminer.com/dicks-sporting-goods...selling-ar-15...a.../2650312 ▾
6 days ago - **Dick's Sporting Goods** announced Wednesday morning that its sister company, Field &
Stream, would discontinue the **sale** of **AR-15** rifles, and that the entire company would raise the ...
"Everybody talks about thoughts and prayers going out to them, and that's great, but that **doesn't** really
do anything.
You visited this page on 3/5/18.

Dick's Sporting Goods says it won't sell assault weapons anymore. - Vox
https://www.vox.com/policy-and-politics/ .../dicks-sporting-goods-parkland-gun-sales ▾
6 days ago - Two weeks after the school shooting in Parkland, Florida, **Dick's Sporting Goods**, one of the
nation's largest **sports** retailers, is ending sales of assault-style rifles in stores. The retailer did the same
thing after the 2012 Sandy Hook Elementary School shooting, but its CEO ...

Dick's Sporting Goods Stops Selling Assault-Style Weapons, Raises ...
https://www.wsj.com/.../dicks-raises-age-for-gun-buyers-will-stop-selling-assault-weapon...
6 days ago - **Dick's Sporting Goods** said it would stop **selling** assault-style rifles, would no longer **sell**
guns to people under 21 and would advocate for more-stringent gun laws ... The gun industry describes
the **AR-15** model and other semiautomatic rifles, such as AK-style weapons, as being modern sporting
rifles.

Dick's Bans Assault Rifle Sales: Cabela's, Bass Still Sell | Money
time.com › Everyday Money › Guns ▾
5 days ago - Cabela's and Bass Pro Shops still **sell** assault rifles, after **Dick's Sporting Goods** says it will
stop **selling** semi-automatic rifles. ... In 2015, all Walmart stores stopped **selling** semi-automatic rifles
like the **AR-15**, the weapon of choice in mass shootings such as those in Sandy Hook, San Bernardino,
Las Vegas, ...
You visited this page on 3/6/18.

Dick's Sporting Goods Ends Assault Rifle Sales, Why It's Low Risk ...

These next several results show the history of the search and how the major news outlets reported it. Notice the names of the outlets and what the headlines communicate. The #2 SERP is the Washington Examiner story – the only critical piece written on the subject (maybe there are more on page 3, 4, 5 and 6 of the Google SERPs, but who looks there anyway?).

Dick's Sporting Goods will no longer sell AR-15 gun, other assault ...
www.syracuse.com/us-news/index.../dicks_sporting_goods_ar-15_assault_rifles.html ▾
6 days ago - **Dick's Sporting Goods** announced Wednesday it is immediately ending sales of the **AR-15**
and similar weapons, along with high-capacity magazines. ... He added that he's a gun owner himself,
but said he **doesn't** want the company stocking assault-style rifles or **selling** guns to shoppers under 21
anymore.

Dick's Sporting Goods, Walmart to Restrict Gun Purchase Age to 21 ...
https://www.rollingstone.com/.../dicks-sporting-goods-to-discontinue-assault-rifle-sale... ▾
6 days ago - Walmart said it had ended the **sale** of some sporting rifles such as the **AR-15** in 2015 and
the company said it **doesn't sell** bump stocks or high-capacity magazines. ***. **Dick's Sporting Goods**
announced Wednesday that it would discontinue its **sale** of assault-style rifles in the aftermath of the
deadly school ..

Walmart and Dick's Raise Minimum Age for Gun Buyers to 21 - The ...
https://www.nytimes.com/.../walmart-and-dicks-major-gun-retailers-will-tighten-rules-on...
6 days ago - Two of the nation's leading gun sellers, Walmart and **Dick's Sporting Goods**, took steps on
Wednesday to limit their sales of firearms, thrusting ... In a news release late Wednesday, Walmart noted
that in 2015 it discontinued the **sale** of high-powered rifles, including **AR-15**-style weapons, in its stores
in the ...

1 2 3 4 5 6 7 8 9 10   Next

Page 2 of the results yields much of the same:

Dick's Sporting Goods Won't Be Selling Assault Rifles Anymore
www.newsweek.com/dicks-sporting-goods-wont-be-selling-semi-automatic-weapons-... ▼
6 days ago - **Dick's Sporting Goods**, one of the U.S.'s largest retailers of sporting equipment, will no longer **sell** assault rifles. ... Stack acknowledged that Cruz had purchased a shotgun at a Dick's outlet in November. Cruz is not accused of using this weapon in the shooting, but a **AR-15** semi-automatic assault rifle.
Missing: doesn

Dick's Sporting Goods Says They Won't Sell 'Assault-Style Weapons ...
https://www.dailywire.com/.../dicks-sporting-goods-says-they-wont-sell-assault-emily-... ▼
6 days ago - In response to the Parkland school shooting, the CEO of athletic retailer **Dick's Sporting Goods**, Edward Stack, told Good Morning America on ... define what constitutes a "high capacity magazine" nor whether "assault weapon" meant the **AR-15** specifically or several different styles of semi-automatic rifles.

Dick's Sporting Goods to stop selling assault-style rifles | Fox Business
www.foxbusiness.com/features/dicks-sporting-goods-to-stop-selling-assault-style-rifles
6 days ago - **Dick's Sporting Goods** Inc. (NYSE:DKS) said on Wednesday it will no longer **sell** assault-style rifles and will ban the **sale** of firearms to people under the age ... a 19-year-old former student who was expelled from the school, allegedly entered the building and killed 17 people, mostly students, with an **AR-15**.

Dick's Sporting Goods will stop selling assault-style rifles - Feb. 28, 2018
money.cnn.com/2018/02/28/news/companies/dicks-weapon-ban/index.html ▼
6 days ago - **Dick's Sporting Goods** said it raise age requirement for firearm sales, stop **selling** military-style semiautomatic weapons in wake of shooting in Parkland ... The Parkland shooter, Nikolas Cruz, did buy a gun at Dick's, but the company said it wasn't the **AR-15**-style rifle that he used in the school shooting.
Missing: doesn

Dick's Sporting Goods CEO on decision to no longer sell assault-style ...
abcnews.go.com/GMA/News/dicks-sporting-goods-ceo-company-longer-sell.../story?

All the major mainstream news outlets weighed in with virtually the same headlines. There were a few outliers like Syracuse University and Vox, but some people might even consider Vox a mainstream outlet these days.

Some interesting questions might be worth exploring, like:

- Why does only one headline challenge Dick's move? (That headline from the Washington Examiner is, by the way, cut off before you can read the word stunt. It's Google's character count limit that's in the works, but at a glance, that headline could be considered neutral or positive.)

- Why does every news organization parrot virtually the same headline? . . . and the same lead?
- What good is a search result if you can't find multiple differing viewpoints on page 1?
- Are there people that think companies like Dick's should stop selling all firearms?
- Does anyone think Dick's should become a private screener of backgrounds? Would that help? Should there be a search result for that?
- If Dick's continues to sell guns, how liable are they for these kinds of school shootings? Handguns kill more people in the U.S. than AR-15s. Should Dick's sell insurance policies to gun owners?
- Should Dick's put some portion of their gun sales profits toward gun violence restitution programs?
- Are there any other good ideas about Dicks and guns?

As you can see, there are lots of potential issues at hand here, but the search results offer very little to the curious.

YouTubers Rule

YouTube, founded in 2005 and bought by Google in 2006, changed the way we watch television. It's interesting, though, how YouTube eventually became more and more like TV as it evolved, with TV commercials and common broadcast show formats, like news, how-to, personality-driven content, interviews, documentaries, comedy shows and the like. In the beginning, it was much more an amateur platform. YouTube is now the place to be for eyeballs and traffic. You can fix your sink there, learn a new language or start your own channel. The possibilities are endless, as long as you don't get banned. Here are some of the early successes on YouTube.

The interesting thing about YouTube is that it took a lot of power away from mainstream TV. However, advertisers eventually flocked to YouTube, and you now have a similar experience, but you're in a bit more control of ad skipping, choosing what to watch and so forth. A TV and DVR experience is similar. But the way cable TV channel guides are structured are a bit clunkier. The guides are getting better, and things like Amazon Prime and Fire TV are improving things.

Gary Vaynerchuk: This kid (I say kid, but he actually came on to the scene as a late 20-something) took his dad's liquor store in New Jersey from a $5 million enterprise to a $60 million e-commerce wine store by leveraging YouTube videos in 2005. This was a time when most people didn't really think much of YouTube and its potential. He created a YouTube channel before there was even the concept of a YouTube channel, describing the science and fun of wine tasting to a new generation of oenophiles. His story is legend, and you may have already heard of him. Take a look at his story by checking Wikipedia.

Casey Neistat: This guy was recently hired by CNN. He started by vlogging (video blogging) about his life and times as a young photographer and video editor. He put his whole life online.

Zoella: This English vlogger and best-selling novelist is known for delivering the goods on beauty and fashion.

Hilah Cooking: This crafty home chef from Austin, Texas took cooking show hype away from the Food Network. Hilah proved that people don't care where they get their cooking shows.

People as Products and Solutions

One interesting way to think about all things advertised is to consider everything a product. People are products, services are products, and actual physical things are products. You may have come across this already. In the age of YouTube, many individuals have staked their claim as "personal brands," which are really just people marketed as a product. Casey Neistat is a product, really. Follow his life, and you'll see that money flows in via various channels (CNN, YouTube maybe, sponsors and clients). But if he's a product, then what are his features? They're soft, aren't they? He inspires and excites and shows you how to adventure and travel. He offers honesty and empathy. He also has product tie-ins for physical products like Samsung phones. He's working for Samsung as a creative leader, and his clients include big brands like Nike, Google, Finn Jewelry and Mercedes-Benz.

People become associated with products. In his early days as an online video marketer, Gary Vaynerchuk blended his personality with wine products. P.T. Barnum became closely associated with his circus product. Suzanne Somers became synonymous with the Thigh Master. Arnold Schwarzenegger will always be remembered as the Terminator. There are hundreds of these examples.

Most of these people make their way into the nightly news programs and network entertainment shows. It's a great way to advertise their solutions. Vaynerchuk did it via Conan O'Brien's show in the early days. Barnum received all kinds of coverage via the news, as did Somers and Aaahnold.

If people can be products, then services can, too. Think about Uber. That's just people picking up and dropping off, like taxis. The internet made the company into something more. Food delivery services became a product. Dating services are a product. Here's where brands and language start to combine into verbs. You Uber to get a ride somewhere, as in "I Ubered to work because my car broke down." You order dinner, as in "Do you want to Postmates some chicken wings tonight?" And, you comment on your dates, as in "That guy you Bumbled last week is a creep."

Think of things as products, and you can see a little behind the curtain that obscures the notion of "help" and makes it into something that takes money from the consumer pocket and delivers it to the company.

This is not to say that any person, service or product is bad. It's just a mindset – an orientation that gets you thinking like an advertiser.

YouTube and Demonetization

Since we've talked about YouTubers a bit here, let's discuss the economics of the platform and some of the realities confronting content producers that decide they want to make a living on YouTube or at least scoop up some advertising dollars via the platform.

The YouTube model, by the way, is in stark contrast to the traditional broadcast TV model where advertisers are courted by sophisticated sales staffs, consider complex Nielsen ratings numbers, and purchase hefty ad buys to get exposure on coveted time slots across the popular networks. YouTube, on the other hand, lets their platform do all the calculating for ad buys, much in the same way the AdWords/AdSense platform works. Advertisers pay for impressions, plays, and insertions into content that is proven popular by the minute, hour, day, month and year. Unlike TV, the metrics and outcomes are very closely tracked within the YouTube back-end platform. You can target specific types of videos and audiences via YouTube, and it can be very granular.

There's a problem, however, if you're a content producer (an advertiser, personality, cause, organization, reviewer, or whatever) that runs astray of Google's human and algorithmic censors. This is going to take some explaining. YouTube (a Google company) is under a lot of pressure to clean up its video feeds. People, governments and organizations across the globe don't want videos on there that show people:

- Making bombs
- Indoctrinating radicals
- Abducting people
- Disseminating hate
- Abusing and exploiting people

Those are legitimate concerns. The trouble comes when gray areas are traversed and free speech is silenced via either YouTube employees or the algorithms that automatically filter and flag videos on the platform. Hundreds of free thinkers that espouse all kinds of ideas that are allowed to be printed in text books and taught in universities have been prevented from sharing their ideas on YouTube and "demonetized" by the censors at that company. What does that mean? Well, let's say you have a YouTube channel with 10 million subscribers and one day you post a video that defends an Islamic group's attack on an Israeli settlement near occupied territories. It's possible and in some cases likely your channel, which brings in thousands of ad dollars every month since you have this huge following, will be blocked by Google and demonetized. You no longer have ads inserted into the pre-roll of your videos, and you don't get any more of that money. Simple. You're done, and you have no recourse. One politically incorrect misstep, and you lose your livelihood.

You can see this explained in a video here:

http://bit.ly/2qX2TFi

Go to the 3:43 minute mark, and you'll get the gist in about 10 seconds.

Here's the summary: The guest, Dr. Jordan Peterson, explains how centrist-conservative or conservative YouTubers have their channels demonetized for the issues and views they choose to discuss. Essentially, Google decides the content is not fit for advertisers. Peterson thinks they do this in an arbitrary way. He advocates for transparency around how this works.

Is this fair? Is it OK since Google and YouTube are private companies that can do whatever they like with their properties? Is YouTube a public space? Should it be regulated as such? TV networks get to choose what they produce and who can advertise on their programming (although there are lots of FCC laws surrounding this practice). Does YouTube get to do the same thing? Is the platform a different animal? Is there an implicit partnership between advertisers and the videos they show up on? Does the advertiser get a say? Can they tell YouTube where they want their ads to show up? These are all big issues that are developing.

Part 6 – Who's Teaching You When You're Watching a Sitcom?

Most people think that situation comedies, those shows that feature families cracking jokes at each other in various situations – like at a bar *Cheers*, at home *Everybody Loves Raymond*, in NYC *Seinfeld* – are created by a writer or a few writers that gather around a table and hash out plots every week.

What they don't realize is that there are dozens of organizations that influence those writers over the course of the season, the year and even over decades. The writers, in many cases, are exposed to the ideas and influence of various influence groups as far back as film school and university writing workshops.

The practice of inserting political, health, diet and social issues into family network programming is often traced back to *All in the Family,* which was written and produced by Norman Lear. Look him up on Wikipedia, and check out his *People for the American Way* organization. He's also head of the foundation that bears his name.

When there were only a few TV channels worth watching – some might argue only three, CBS, ABC and NBC – the networks had an oligopoly on the attention of U.S. TV viewers. So several foundations and causes took advantage of that in order to promote certain views and habits among the viewership.

One good early example of this was described in a report referred to as the MCD report (for Media Citizens and Democracy). The report is titled

---

But who cares? Who watches TV anyway these days? Certainly not kids!

Influence over the populace via network, cable and other broadcast outlets (including radio) didn't just go away because the eyeballs are now focused on the internet, gaming and apps rather than the boob tube.

The same forces are at work when you're playing a game, using Instagram, or browsing videos on YouTube.

Media companies are just now scrambling to reproduce their ad models and influence models, and layer that onto web-based and app-based properties.

The "kids" think they're immune to the advertising, but the same old pitch strategies and tactics keep showing up – just in other forms – via different channels.

How Pro-Social Messages Make Their Way Into Entertainment Programming, and it was compiled and written by Mandy Shaivitz of the USC Annenberg School of Communications' Norman Lear Center, which is connected to the foundation of that same name.

Here's some of the rationale behind the report, as stated in the opening paragraphs:

> "The past two decades have seen an upsurge in the use of entertainment programming for the dissemination of pro-social messages. Since the early 1980s, more than twenty organizations have appeared in Hollywood with the purpose of altering or improving portrayals of particular issues in television and film. Certainly these organizations and campaigns assert that they are necessary as countless messages concerning medicine, public health, law and government among others, are embedded in entertainment media and because of the truism that people learn from the programming they watch.
>
> "The present work provides a review of the literature and practices of organizations that seek to work with the entertainment industry through different means; the organizations are typically referenced as "entertainment education" or "advocacy groups," although the terms are often interchangeable. The key elements of interest, however, are the strategies and activities employed by such efforts, along with measures and evidence of success.
>
> "While there is a great deal of information-sharing among the various organizations that seek to work with the entertainment industry to influence content, this information is not readily available to the public. Organizations hoping to enter the field

of media advocacy face a sizeable, time-consuming initiation and development process in order to get "up and running." This project reviews the activities of nineteen representative groups and presents suggested techniques for working with the entertainment industry."

The report goes on to describe how a popular 1970's show – *Happy Days* (ask your parents) – changed the behavior of the public in a very significant and impactful way. In one episode, the cool character on the show, a 50's greaser and motorcycle dude named Fonzie visited the local library and received a library card. The report notes that libraries around the U.S.A. reported record numbers of new library card requests for an extensive time period after the episode had aired.

Happy Days ran from 1974 to 1984, and *All in the Family* ran from 1971 to 1979. These shows were demonstrating and spearheading what would become common practice by the time the *How Pro-Social Messages Make Their Way Into Entertainment Programming* report was put together in 2003. [This year is an estimate. The report itself, which is available on the Internet, does not carry a copyright date.] The practice would later become known as *media advocacy*. That's the more broad term which the writer/producer/director influence falls under.

The report is interesting. We'll pull some quotes from it the end of this section. Let's take a look at some of the advocacy organizations detailed within the report first. The following descriptions come directly from the report, verbatim:

- **Population Communications International:** PCI has chosen to concentrate its efforts on soap operas since the longevity of these programs provides an opportunity for viewers to identify with characters, thus allowing for greater likelihood of adapting the modeled behavior (Albert Bandura's Social Learning theories).

And, as new characters join the show, there is occasion for a natural and unforced introduction of new issues

- **HARVARD ALCOHOL PROJECT:** Entertainment programming: meetings held by Center staff with over 250 decision-makers from all the leading primetime shows, an action supported by SAG and WGA, west. The result: the casual insertion of Designated Driver messages into scripts of popular shows like The Cosby Show, Cheers and LA Law, with characters modeling behavior in a subtle way.

[My commentary: Harvard Alcohol Project also completed all kinds of other work – all admirable – but we just don't hear about it as media consumer. These include public service announcements (PSAs) with the President of the U.S. speaking about alcohol and designated driver issues, and feature articles and editorials in all the major publications and news networks. What we don't know is if there are payments involved. Does government money flow to studios to get access? Who knows? It requires more digging. Some of these PSAs ran 10-20 times a week during prime time programming (prime time is typically considered 8PM – 11PM). That's expensive ad time.]

- **HOLLYWOOD IMMUNIZATION PROJECT**: Story ideas were collected through qualitative interviews with health professionals and through online news databases searches, and they were summarized into simple paragraphs with headlines, called "story lines." These materials were mailed to industry decision-makers along with clippings, lists of experts and a catalogue containing photos of various immunization posters.
  - Four criteria for working in the storytelling medium were established:
    - "true stories about immunizations or vaccines and their impact on real people would help to

establish the authenticity of the issues and the project"

- ■ "although [they] could not control the content of television scripts, [they] could favorably influence industry gatekeepers and decision makers by presenting ideas with entertainment value"
- ■ "arranged stories that they would fit into the context of entertainment programs"
- ■ "as shows typically focus on characters and their relationships, and characters represent certain socio-demographic groups, [they] arranged the stories in the following categories to maximize their relevance: children, teens, adults, pregnant women, controversies and myths and misconceptions"

- **CHILDREN NOW**, Children and the Media Project: Children Now's Children and the Media program was created with the goal of improving messages that children receive via news and entertainment media. For the past four years, the program has focused on race, class and gender issues.
  - ○ Strategies and Activities: Children and the Media's general activities include research, outreach to media leaders and policy work. The project:
    - ■ develops national youth opinion surveys and content analyses that assess the media's impact on children
    - ■ holds briefings for television writers and producers whose programs deal with children's real-life issues
    - ■ runs symposia for media industry leaders to discuss how their work affects children

■ analyzes the messages media send children

■ has "developed public policies to improve television for children," "lobbied for federal legislation requiring V-chips in new TVs" as well as "testified before the U.S. Senate Commerce Committee on ratings survey findings"

[My commentary: This is an interesting one considering we're in the age of YouTube everywhere and unmitigated access to any kind of porn and violence on the internet. There was a time when TV manufacturers were being pressured to put these V-chips into their TVs. The chips put viewing restrictions on certain channels so children couldn't see them. Some sets may have been built with these in them.]

Recently, the project has addressed issues of diversity and media representation of people of color. In order to do so, Children and the Media:

- convened an advisory board to plan its research
- conducted a national poll of children's perception of race in the media and reviewed relevant academic literature (Using Social Learning Theory to guide their research, the researchers found that many ethnic groups are underrepresented and this has a detrimental effect on the self-esteem of children)

[My commentary: These are all very altruistic and well-intended endeavors, but as we'll see later, this is a slippery slope when you put foundations and advocacy groups in positions of power relative to networks, producers, directors, writers and even actors.]

- **S.T.A.R.S. PROJECT** (Seeking Tobacco Alternatives with Realistic Solutions) : Somewhat unique to this project, S.T.A.R.S. has worked with a formal evaluation group from the UCLA School of Public Health to document the effectiveness of their program. UCLA has conducted impact evaluations of Scene Smoking at both the premiere and the AFI Speakers Bureau and determined that the sixty-minute documentary changed viewers' attitudes regarding responsibility of actors, directors and producers in depicting smoking in film.   In the past three years, the project has met successfully its goals of establishing long-lasting relationships with members of the entertainment industry, of achieving positive and extensive visibility and encouraging entertainment professionals to reflect on the need and potential impact of making the choice to depict smoking in film.

[My commentary: This kind advocacy attempts to work for the good of society. What's interesting, however, is that it took decades to get to this point. Smoking was portrayed in movies and on TV as the ultimate cool from the very beginning. James Dean, Bette Davis, Clark Gable and all kinds of other famous actors smoked in movies without much care by the public or the companies producing the movies. Tobacco companies like R.J. Reynolds and Philip Morris actually paid to have their products promoted in movies and TV by having actors smoke cigarettes on screen. Not until the late 1960's and early 1970's did the public begin to react to earlier research on the dangers of tobacco and nicotine. Then public pressure groups like S.T.A.R.S began to force this kind of lifestyle advertising out of entertainment. My only question here is where does this end? Could sugar consumption be banned in movies? New York City Mayor Bill De Blasio banned the sale of large format soft drinks in the city. It's possible. Could sex scenes be forced out of movies? In the 1950's and earlier directors were not allowed to show male and female actors in the same bed. True. Again where does it end? And are you really a free person if you don't have the ability to choose (or watch!) your own behaviors without censure from public groups? Where do we draw the line between healthy advocacy and the impingement on free thought and actions? Granted, you don't have to watch movies that have smoking, alcohol, drugs or sex in them. That's your choice. But do directors and other creatives need to be policed or bribed by advocacy groups? This is a nice little debate.

Exercise: Choose one side of this debate and bring some bulleted talking points to class so we can discuss.

- **THE MEDIA PROJECT**: The result of a collaborative effort between Advocates for Youth and the Kaiser Family Foundation, The Media Project provides current, socially relevant and accurate information about sexual health (family planning, sexuality and reproductive health) to entertainment industry professionals.
  - Once meetings are set, The Media Project attempts to empower their hosts and convince them of their influence to affect what's shown in programming and what children eventually see on television. The Project works with approximately twenty television shows on an ongoing basis and regularly records their programs to evaluate the success of their meetings. In order to acknowledge shows for incorporating the appropriate information into their story lines, The Media Project sends praising letters calling attention to their positive actions.
  - While The Media Project has conducted quantitative online viewer polls that have illustrated a change in knowledge and behavior—because it is difficult to identify a causal relationship between what children see on television and their attitudes and behavior— most of their evaluation is anecdotal. Examples of evaluation include:
    - maintaining a record of shows that have applied information received through meetings, briefings and mailings
    - compiling an ongoing list of organizations which with they have maintained an enduring relationship

- conducting focus groups and informal interviews with teens to collect feedback on the work the Project creates (such as videos on teen issues)

[My commentary: This one is interesting. They note that it's difficult to show causation between TV viewing and behavior, and then they show evaluation bullets that are anything but anecdotal. They just watch over and meet with shows and then conduct the odd focus group with teens to get feedback on their work. This is strange. The question here is, what kinds of relationships and sexual depiction does this group approve of? Do they advocate for certain types of affection-depiction? Do they advise against other kinds? What's their end game? Safer kids? Puritan ideals? Pan-sexual society? I'm sure we could find out more with some digging and research. Also, why aren't writers and directors allowed to show their creative works without pressure from these groups? Some are, I know, but they don't always get the opportunity to be on network television. They usually show up in edgy indie movies and the like.]

- **ENTERTAINMENT INDUSTRIES COUNCIL**: EIC coined the phrase "depiction suggestions" and has developed two full volumes of depiction books; one volume covers drug, alcohol and tobacco use, and the other focuses on gun violence and safety. In addition, the group creates numerous individual topic fact sheets with suggestions about how to include these issues into storylines.
  - Strategies and Activities: The group focuses its attention on four areas:
    - "First Draft"—a technical resource service that provides information on request
    - "Spotlight on Depiction"—writers' resources, debriefings (both information-based, smaller briefings and dialogue-based, larger forums with industry members) and news briefs

213

■ "Generation Next"—educational resources
for film school students, which includes
film school seminars, access to First Draft
and other written resources and a
fellowship writing program that matches
students with experts and creative mentors
■ PRISM—annual awards that recognize
accurate and current depictions of drug,
tobacco and alcohol use in film and
television

[My comments: This one's self-explanatory and like the other
organizations above. What's interesting is how they guide their mission by
conducting seminars and writing programs to further their goals. They're
starting early in the process (film school) to teach aspiring writers and
directors how Hollywood works.]

The entire MCD report sums up their aims in tracking the
organizations mentioned above as follows:

"The project aims to develop an effective message and
communications strategy that will engage citizens, especially young
Americans, in government and democracy, through the examination of the
portrayal of government and public service in entertainment media. The
project's final report summarizes its findings on effective methods used by
advocacy groups to influence entertainment content."

That's from the intro to the report.

These are the organizations behind the report:

The Council for Excellence in Government	The Norman Lear Center
The Council for Excellence in Government works to improve the performance of government at all levels	Based at the USC Annenberg School for Communication, the Norman Lear Center is a multidisciplinary research and public policy center exploring implications of the

and government's place in the lives and esteem of American citizens. With its experienced staff, network of experts and members and diverse partners, the Council helps to create stronger public sector leadership and management, driven by innovation and focused on results; and increased citizen confidence and participation in government, through better understanding of government and its role. Founded in 1982, the organization is nonpartisan, nonprofit and national in scope.

convergence of entertainment, commerce, and society. On the USC campus, the Lear Center builds bridges between eleven schools whose faculty study aspects of entertainment, media and culture. Beyond campus, it bridges the gap between the entertainment industry and academia, and between them and the public. Through scholarship and research; through its programs of visiting fellows, conferences, public events, and publications; and in its attempts to illuminate and repair the world, the Lear Center works to be at the forefront of discussion and practice in the field.

Interestingly, the Norman Lear foundation is a very liberal group (most of Hollywood is known as such, but you can look up Norman Lear comments online and in YouTube videos to see what he's about – he's neither good nor bad, but he has a well-defined agenda). With this advocacy in mind, you have to ask yourself some questions: What do they mean by "illuminate and repair the world?" Through sitcoms? Through night time dramas? Seinfeld? Cheers? *The Cosby Show*? Modern Family? How exactly does that happen via a passive drama and comedy consumption mechanism like the boob tube?

Our only conclusion can be that by shaping public opinion through fictional portrayals, these groups intend to "illuminate and repair" societal issues. Are we defining propaganda here? How does it work? We condition the thoughts of viewers first, then government actions become more palatable? Or, are viewers encouraged to activism and government influence via direct vote and/or protest and referendum/proposition avenues? Which comes first. We suspect it's a combination thereof. However the former scenario seems more likely since activism by TV viewers seems a bit of a stretch. Does your couch potato friend seem like the type to march on Washington D.C.? Maybe. Maybe not. It seems more likely that the agendas promoted on TV would prepare the population for certain decisions which are made outside of their purview or direct influence.

By the way, if you want to look up political contributions (by party, PAC and other data) on each of these foundations and influence groups, you can do so at https://www.opensecrets.org.

Mass Media Persona Profile

There's a certain type of person that's becoming extinct as digital media proliferates and mass media fragmentation continues. People are cutting cords, kids are watching media via YouTube (they're watching very targeted, long-tail, niche channels), and major network shows continue to see their ratings fall or flatten. The persona that's becoming extinct as a result could be called the mass media consumer.

You probably know a few. They watch network TV shows, some Netflix shows, some Showtime and HBO shows, and a handful of cable TV shows that are highly popular. Shows like:

- Homeland
- Game of Thrones
- Unreal
- The Big Bang Theory
- The Walking Dead
- Grey's Anatomy
- This Is Us
- NCIS
- Saturday Night Live (SNL)
- Modern Family
- Black-ish
- Scandal
- Stranger Things

What's interesting about this persona or psychographic profile is that they're soaking in most if not all of the Lear Center/Annenberg-type content. They get all the major themes and persuasion related to:

- Gender issues
- Gun control
- Women's issues
- Immigration
- Foreign policy
- Homosexuality and LGBTQQIAAP
- Animal rights
- Veganism and diet
- Family dynamics
- And more. .

And remember, these social and political positions are developed by a very small group of people and are baked into the popular mass-media programming. Some of these people do not watch regular news broadcasts, and they form their opinions about issues via osmosis from these shows. Don't take this word osmosis lightly, either. We form beliefs based on the types of media we consume and the specific messaging that's baked into that media. You are what you eat, in other words. There's no getting around it. It's the reason why people who go on news and media diets feel lighter and clearer in the head after they've logged weeks away from the noise of TV, internet and mobile phone apps.

Those from this group who do watch news programming tend to consume it via the popular, mass-media channels like the big three broadcasters (ABC, CBS, NBC) and CNN and Fox News. They get the party lines and not much else.

Exercise: Go through your list of friends and family members and see if you can identify any mass-media types. Don't call them out on it, of course. Nobody wants to be pegged and stereotyped based on their behaviors. Once you have a couple in mind, see if you can put their political and social views into a summary. Bring these summaries to class, and we'll discuss them anonymously. We'll see if we can identify salient personas and identify trends. Use the list above to jot down some of their positions on those issues.

YouTuber Redux – Truman Show Didn't Get it Right

A lot of media critics and futurists get a kick out of comparing the common state of things to the 1998 movie *The Truman Show*. In that movie, some hapless schmuck gets picked out of a baby lottery to be manipulated by TV show directors and producers – including a wacky cast of actors that keep him in the dark.

If you think about it, however, the prognosticators got it kind of backwards. The public didn't need to be duped into anything. There's no grand reality show that will grab all of our worldwide attention. No baby needs to be adopted into a studio.

The YouTubers did a reverse – tricking Hollywood into featuring them after they'd gained notoriety all on their own! Neistat got a deal with CNN. Vaynerchuk cashes checks from the NHL, Chase, Anheuser-Busch, Amazon and major wineries that he once featured on his Wine Library YouTube channel. All kinds of beauty, travel and lifestyle personalities built businesses on their YouTube popularity and attracted advertisers and YouTube pre-roll ads to their channels.

It all happened organically. No Hollywood studio intervened or crafted the strategy. Some definitely piggybacked onto the trend, and the major talent agencies inserted themselves into the YouTube playground. But the phenomenon took off by itself. Thousands of popular YouTubers cropped up over a 5-10 year period, crowning themselves "Trumans" by producing compelling videos, offering value and entertainment to viewers, and drawing people into their lives.

This is something that caught Hollywood and NYC totally off guard. In the past, agents, producers and directors selected talent from auditioning actors and popular personalities from within the industry. Even the daytime talk show hosts came from within the industry. Oprah came from movies. Ellen came from stand-up comedy. Whoopi came from movies and comedy. Phil Donahue came from news production and radio announcing, and Charlie Rose came from news.

For our purposes, these developments are both interesting and important to follow. Moving forward, we should expect to see Hollywood and NYC attempt to insert their influence and agendas into this new crop of media influencers. Many of the big YouTubers already have contracts with the big agencies like Creative Artists Agency (CAA), William Morris, and International Creative Management (ICM). Some big video gamers are getting into the talent system, as well. Once these people become involved with the institutional players, we should expect them to play ball with the usual suspects in programming creation – including Lear, Annenberg and that whole system of writers, directors and producers who shepherd the major social and political themes of our era.

Can Primetime Dramas Shape Your View of Government?

In 2004, the aforementioned Lear Center examined how people perceive our government, government workers and civic themes. Their surveys and interviews found that, indeed, TV education campaigns (the kind that insert themes into shows via these advocacy groups like the Norman Lear Foundation) influence people to change their minds about topics, motivate them to action, and generally pique their interest in government topics. A large portion of the people they surveyed seemed to replace any news consumption or current events understandings with this diet of TV information via fictionalized entertainment programming.

If you'd like to examine the whole thing, here's the link to the report:

http://bit.ly/2qYD1ZK

PRINCETON ANNENBERG
CHANGING CHANNELS
ENTERTAINMENT

And, here are just a few tidbits for your examination and amusement. These passages are under the subheading *"TV as a Source of Information about Government."*

> "The medium of television has a major influence on people's view of the federal government. Among all those age 18-49, about as many say that what they see on television matters more than personal experience in determining their view of government as say personal experience is the more important factor (44% vs. 45%). The subgroup most likely to say television is the bigger influence are those who do not regularly use any news source, be it TV or radio, newspapers or magazines, or the Internet. Fifty-seven percent of the non-regular consumers of news outlets, compared with 43% of regular consumers, say what they see on TV has more impact than personal experiences on their view of the federal government. Demographically, women are more likely than men (49% vs. 39%) and those with no college are more likely than the college educated (50% vs. 39%) to say TV is more important. No significant differences are found by age."

Let's let that sink in. Or maybe just re-read it. This is pretty crazy.

Here are the shows the Lear Center included in their sampling for this particular survey:

- Law & Order
- JAG
- The West Wing
- Third Watch
- Boston Public
- Judging Amy
- The District
- Alias
- The Agency
- Mr. Sterling

If the numbers in these surveys are still holding up (granted this is from 2004 and viewing habits probably changed quite a bit), then we're allowing screenwriters and the advocacy groups that influence them to significantly shape our understanding of how government, legislation, Miranda law, search and seizure, police actions, court rulings, congressional debate and a number of other critical civic functions happen.

The report also found that these primetime dramas had more influence over viewers than late night comedy shows (like David Letterman and Jay Leno – who were the Jimmy Fallons and Jimmy Kimmels of their day). One could argue that, in our sound bite, short attention span states of 2018, the late night talk show hosts have more influence, and that their influence and politicization has changed over the years. In the age of Trump and Hillary, you have much more vitriolic and impassioned pleas by what were once hosts driven by sensibilities more in tune with stand-up comedians (as opposed to political commentators).

More from the report:

"The TV viewing public is divided about how accurately entertainment TV shows in general portray government and people who work in government. About four in 10 adults under age 50 say such portrayals are mostly (39%) or very (2%) accurate, while an equal number report that such portrayals are mostly (33%) or very (8%) inaccurate. But when asked about specific types of government-themed shows, the public gives a range of accuracy ratings, with shows with judicial themes getting the highest marks.

"Regular viewers of target shows are more likely than regular viewers of non-target shows to perceive TV depictions of government as credible. A majority (58%) say the way entertainment TV shows portray government and people who work in government is accurate, compared with 44% of those who regularly watch non-target shows. Target show viewers who are loyal to two or more of the target shows are especially impressed with the depictions; 64% indicate the shows provide realistic portrayals."

I'm going to go out on a limb here and pose a couple of questions. Could the divide that's described above be the "two Americas" you see referenced in the press these days? Could there be a media-influenced public and a media-immune public that are divided along ideological lines?

By the way, this report and the shows are dated. That's clear. Yes, habits have changed and we consume more media on the web. But Netflix still runs these old shows. They're quite popular with the binge-watchers. And there are a whole new crop of dramas that people consume by the trough-load, including *House of Cards, Game of Thrones, Stranger Things, The Walking Dead, The West Wing, Grey's Anatomy, The Handmaid's Tale, Narcos, Sense8, 13 Reasons Why* and more. These are all influenced by the same media advocacy groups.

This entry from Wikipedia about *Sense8* tips you off to the ongoing practice:

> "The show aims to explore subjects that its creators feel have not been emphasized in many science fiction shows to date, such as politics, identity, sexuality, gender and religion."

That's a line right out of the Norman Lear Center documents.

The phenomenon has not gone away. I know we always come back to this point, but I think it's important. As much as young people think they're choosing to watch whatever they want, the large media powers infiltrate their viewing lives in some way. I know I'm not speaking about all of you, but there are large portions of the youth population that consume traditional media. They just access it via different channels. Netflix, HBO, Hulu and Amazon are much more popular today than the ABC/CBS/NBC triumvirate of yesteryear (add PBS, too), but the same producers, writers, directors and advocacy groups are behind the productions.

Product Placement in Movies, TV, Games and Apps

This one is pretty simple, and recent data has shown that it doesn't work so well. So, what is product placement? The best way to witness it as a lampoon is in the old 90's movie *Wayne's World.* Here's the clip from YouTube.

http://bit.ly/2r5i9QL

The studio production is paid by advertisers to place branded products – preferably in the hands of stars – into the movie or TV show. This translates to video games and apps, as well. You get it. The clip above is just pure bliss, because they tease the whole idea of product placement while cashing the checks. That was a huge, blockbuster movie at the time, and they certainly raked it in from Doritos, Pepsi, Nuprin, Reebok and Pizza Hut. By the way, all those brands – even the ones on the table in the first frame – are Pepsi (or more accurately Yum! Brands) products. That was a single ad buy that purchased eyeballs for a half dozen products. Genius!

Here's the data on product placement returns. Some people call this embedded marketing.

If product placement doesn't work so well, then what's the alternative?

The best way to describe the alternative would be *behavior placement*. When characters that are emulated or looked up to in movies, TV shows and video games display certain behaviors, the viewers/players tend to model those behaviors. This is a proven psychological phenomenon in popular culture. People smoked because of James Dean and Humphrey Bogart. They flocked to discos and country music bars because of John Travolta (*Stayin' Alive* and *Urban Cowboy*), and they pounded tropical drinks in all-inclusive spa get-aways because of Tom Cruise in *Cocktail*.

Advertisers know this, and they "consult" with movie productions to get specific behaviors and their corresponding products (though not overtly branded) into the production. In this sense, the advertisers work more as lobbyists more than individual product advertisers. It's like the almond lobby that hustles Washington D.C. to make regulations more favorable to California almond farmers. These influence groups – think alcohol, tobacco, gaming, gambling, firearms, aspirational travel, media, politics – insert themselves into the production process to model behaviors that increase sales in their particular market. Think that's crazy?

What you can discern from this activity is that advertisers and their production counterparts are dedicated to the long game. They aren't especially enamored with the quick hits that in-production product placements can generate, but they are keenly interested in the kinds of long term behavioral trends that movies, games and TV can portray. They want specific demographics to think, care and obsess about specific FUD-A topics, ideas, issues, motivations and their solutions.

Remember the model is pretty simple: Stoke a fear, uncertainty or doubt. Build a story around it. Make it aspirational, if necessary. Then provide the product solution to the dilemma. Over the decades, I've written hundreds of "case studies" that leverage this exact format. It's classic advertising, classic PR, and classic persuasion. It's also classic screenplay writing, although that's a bit more nuanced.

Exercise: Go to your DVR, phone, tablet, TV or PC and pull up some of your favorite movies or shows. Can you find some examples of product or behavior placement? If so, whip out your phone and record some of them for us. Bring them to class, and we'll have a look at what kinds of examples we've compiled. And we'll have fun going through all of them!

Part 7 – ALT-News

Alternative Networks

Thanks to the internet age, you don't have to watch *any* mass media that's popular in this country. You don't have to be force-fed American propaganda, conservative talking points, CIA PR campaigns, progressive smears or billion-dollar sponsored news content that's never going to offer edgy, controversial or alternative views.

This is kind of a two-edged sword. There are so many news outlets out there that you could believe and support *practically anything!* Unfortunately, there are not a lot of unbiased media outlets out there that can help you make fair decisions about issues and even scientific findings. That could be one of the big conundrums of our time: How to discern truth (or approximate truth) in a theater of smoke, misdirection, lies, hopes, fabrications, big-money ad buys and political corruption.

We're not going to solve that one just yet . . . or maybe never. The obfuscation and profit game is nothing new by historical standards.

What we can do, however, is take a look at some of the unique alternative news outlets and some of their backers. These publishers and media platforms are backed by money, of course. There's very little out there that isn't. Nobody works for free. They have political and ideological backing. Yet they do provide great new angles of thought and discourse which are absolutely not available via traditional media channels in the U.S. Their different approaches to the same exact issues we're dealing with here provide insights and perspective. . . if not answers. They also offer international viewpoints that are simply not covered in any depth in American media.

Al Jazeera: This from Wikipedia – "Al Jazeera is a state-funded broadcaster in Doha, Qatar, owned by the Al Jazeera Media Network. Initially launched as an Arabic news and current-affairs satellite TV channel, Al Jazeera has since expanded into a network with several outlets, including the Internet and specialty television channels in multiple languages.

"Al Jazeera Media Network is a major global news organization, with 80 bureaus around the world. The original Al Jazeera Arabic channel's willingness to broadcast dissenting views, for example on call-in shows, created controversies in the Arab States of the Persian Gulf. The station gained worldwide attention following the outbreak of the war in Afghanistan, when its office there was the only channel to cover the war live.

"The network is owned by the government of Qatar. Al Jazeera Media Network has stated that they are editorially independent from the government of Qatar as the network is funded through loans and grants rather than government subsidies. Some have accused Al Jazeera of being a propaganda outlet for the Qatari government. The network is sometimes perceived to have mainly Islamist perspectives, promoting the Muslim Brotherhood, and having a pro-Sunni and an anti-Shia bias in its reporting of regional issues. However, Al Jazeera insists it covers all sides of a debate; it says it presents Israel's view, Iran's view and even aired videos released by Osama bin Laden. In June 2017, the Saudi, Emirati, Bahraini, and Egyptian governments demanded the closure of the news station as one of thirteen demands made to Qatar during the 2017 Qatar Crisis. Other media networks have spoken out in support of the network. According to *The Atlantic*, Al Jazeera presents a far more moderate, Westernized face than Islamic jihadism or rigid Sunni orthodoxy, and though the network has been criticized as "an 'Islamist' stalking horse" it actually features "very little specifically religious content in its broadcasts"

"**Al Jazeera America** (AJAM) [closed in 2016 – see below] was an American basic cable and satellite news television channel owned by the Al Jazeera Media Network. The channel was launched on August 20, 2013 to compete with CNN, HLN, MSNBC, Fox News, and in certain markets, RT America.

"The channel was headquartered and run from studios on the first floor of the Manhattan Center in New York City. It also had a total of 12 bureaus located in places such as Washington, D.C., at the channel's D.C. studios at the Newseum and Al Jazeera's D.C. hub, Chicago, Detroit, Nashville, Los Angeles, Seattle, New Orleans, Dallas, Denver, Miami, and San Francisco (former headquarters of Current TV and current headquarters of online channel AJ+).

"On January 14, 2016, the Al Jazeera Media Network announced that it would shut down Al Jazeera America's cable TV and digital operations on April 30, 2016, citing plummeting oil prices and the highly competitive nature of the American media market. . . During its two-year history, Al Jazeera America won several media awards including the Peabody, Emmy, and Shorty Awards and citations from groups such as the National Association of Black Journalists and Native American Journalism. However, the network experienced low viewership ratings, averaging between 20,000 and 40,000 viewers on a typical day."

Democracy Now!: From Wikipedia – "*Democracy Now!* is an hour-long American TV, radio and internet news program hosted by journalists Amy Goodman and Juan González. The show, which airs live each weekday at 08:00 ET, is broadcast on the internet and by over 1,400 radio and television stations worldwide. The program combines news reporting, interviews, investigative journalism and political commentary with an eye toward documenting social movements, struggles for justice and the effects of American foreign policy. While described as progressive by fans as well as critics, the show's executive producer rejects that label, calling the program a global newscast that has "people speaking for themselves". The outlet is funded entirely through contributions from listeners, viewers, and foundations and does not accept advertisers, corporate underwriting or government funding."

Even though Democracy Now! goes to great pains to describe themselves as funded only by certain entities, you need to be aware that they're funded by foundations. The fact that they don't accept advertisements does not mean that there's no hidden influence behind the program. Foundations promote everything from energy policy to specific social causes. (By the way, don't you hate companies that put punctuation into their names/logos?)

Here's how Democracy Now! describes themselves (from their About Us page): "As an independent news program, Democracy Now! is audience-supported, which means that our editorial independence is never compromised by corporate or government interests. Since our founding in 1996, Democracy Now! has held steadfast to our policy of not accepting government funding, corporate sponsorship, underwriting or advertising revenue."

They do, however, accept money from foundations, which have government, non-profit and corporate fingerprints all over them! Nice try.

The Intercept: From Wikipedia - "The Intercept is an online news publication dedicated to what it describes as "adversarial journalism". It is supported financially by First Look Media Works. Its editors are Betsy Reed, Glenn Greenwald, and Jeremy Scahill. The publication initially served as a platform to report on the documents released by Edward Snowden, with the long-term goal of producing journalism across a wide range of issues.

Here's some juicy stuff, also from Wikipedia:

"The Intercept's first published story was an in-depth report in February 2014 about the NSA's involvement in the U.S. targeted killing program, which detailed the flawed methods that are used to locate targets for lethal drone strikes, resulting in the deaths of innocent people. This was followed by an article containing new aerial photographs of the NSA, NRO, and NGA headquarters.

"In March 2014, The Intercept published leaked documents from Edward Snowden showing that the National Security Agency was building a system to infect potentially millions of computers around the world with malware. The report included a top-secret NSA animation showing how the agency disguised itself as a Facebook server in order to hack into computers for surveillance. The story reportedly prompted Facebook founder and CEO Mark Zuckerberg to telephone President Obama and complain about NSA's surveillance. Zuckerberg later wrote in a blog post: "I've called President Obama to express my frustration over the damage the government is creating for all of our future.""

Interesting stuff, ay? Not the kind of news you'd find on the nightly newscasts.

Contrast this with how The Intercept describes itself (from their site's About Us page): "The Intercept is an award-winning news organization that covers national security, politics, civil liberties, the environment, international affairs, technology, criminal justice, the media, and more. The Intercept gives its journalists the editorial freedom and legal support they need to pursue investigations that expose corruption and injustice wherever they find it and hold the powerful accountable.

"eBay founder and philanthropist Pierre Omidyar provided the funding to launch The Intercept and continues to support it through First Look Media Works, a nonprofit organization."

RT (Formerly Russia Today): From Wikipedia – "RT is a Russian international television network funded by the Russian government. It operates cable and satellite television channels directed to audiences outside of Russia, as well as providing Internet content in various languages, including English, Spanish and Russian."

By the way, the U.S.A. does the same exact thing, and it's called Voice of America.

"RT International, based in Moscow, presents around-the-clock news bulletins, documentaries, talk shows, debates, sports news, and cultural programmes that it says provide "a Russian viewpoint on major global events".

"RT has been frequently described as a propaganda outlet for the Russian government and its foreign policy. RT has also been accused of spreading disinformation by news reporters, including some former RT reporters. [I don't know what that last sentence means. I guess they're saying that former RT reporters backed up that accusation. Bad sentence structure.]

"The creation of RT was a part of a larger public relations effort by the Russian Government in 2005 that was intended to improve the image of Russia abroad. . . At the time of RT's founding, RIA Novosti director Svetlana Mironyuk stated: "Unfortunately, at the level of mass consciousness in the West, Russia is associated with three words: communism, snow and poverty," and added "we would like to present a more complete picture of life in our country.""

This bit is from RT's About Us page on their site: "RT creates news with an edge for viewers who want to Question More. RT covers stories overlooked by the mainstream media, provides alternative perspectives on current affairs, and acquaints international audiences with a Russian viewpoint on major global events."

Voice of America: From Wikipedia – "Voice of America (VOA) is a U.S. government-funded international news source that serves as the United States federal government's official institution for non-military, external broadcasting. As the largest U.S. international broadcaster, VOA produces digital, TV, and radio content in more than 40 languages which it distributes to affiliate stations around the globe. Primarily viewed by foreign audiences, VOA programming has an influence on public opinion abroad regarding the United States and its leaders."

Here's the zinger, also from Wikipedia: "Some scholars and commentators consider Voice of America to be a form of propaganda. In a response to United States Department of Justice requesting RT to register as a foreign agent under the Foreign Agents Registration Act, Russia's Justice Ministry also labeled Voice of America and Radio Free Europe/Radio Liberty as foreign agents in December 2017."

Don't you love an open and free internet!?!

From the VOA website's About Us page: "Since its creation in 1942, Voice of America has been committed to providing comprehensive coverage of the news and telling audiences the truth. Through World War II, the Cold War, the fight against global terrorism, and the struggle for freedom around the globe today, VOA exemplifies the principles of a free press.

"VOA is part of the Broadcasting Board of Governors, the government agency that oversees all non-military, U.S. international broadcasting. It is funded by the U.S. Congress."

So that's what some of your tax dollars are up to.

RANT! Why Does News Analysis Fail So Often?

Why does news analysis fail so often? We're not talking about reporting – they fail at that, too. We're talking about the examination of issues, events and crises via on-air "experts" who are supposed to get to the bottom of things and give the dumb public some better insight than we'd get from a gossip session down at the corner market.

You'd think it's not all that difficult.

There's one simple answer: Networks and news organizations are not in the news business. You heard that right. Their *business* model is designed to help large corporations sell their products. You don't see mom and pop stores or Etsy shops selling on network TV. Once you watch enough network news with a critical eye, you'll see that there's a big player in the mix. Patented prescription drugs.

And people wonder why there's an opioid problem in the U.S. Interestingly, the U.S. is the only country that promotes and allows ads for big, expensive patented drugs (remember, the business of America is business – thank you Calvin Coolidge). TV pharmaceutical ads became prominent in the mid-1990's. The first ad on TV appeared in 1983. It was promoting the prescription pain reliever Rufen, which was a competitor of Motrin - both ibuprofen.

Yes, there are doctors, the government, addicts, clinics, pharmacies, and big pharma companies to blame for the epidemic. But the tip of the spear is the media. They control the message, and they're not going to kill their golden goose. Pharma pays the bills. We could go into great detail here about how a lot of opium/heroin addicts get started with Oxycodone and other flavors of expensive, pharmaceutical-grade morphine, but we won't. You can read lots about that elsewhere. It's also unknown whether suggestions about the efficacy and prevalence of drug ads on TV shape addict or drug user behavior. The whole gateway drug phenomenon is debatable, as well (again, a topic for another day).

Since the media controls popular reporting on these issues, you'd have to think they wouldn't blame themselves for the problem. That's not good business. You'll see the media cover stories about price gouging, but in light of what we covered about Tamiflu earlier, that could be the way they get more ad buys through the door. They never really take on a crusade against price gouging, however. *Follow the money*. They'll also report on the most brutal and egregious examples of prescription drug tragedies, but they usually conclude the reports with an attitude that says, "Gosh, that's too bad. Something should be done."

Exercise: Record a national evening newscast on ABC, NBC, CBS, Fox News or CNN and count the number of pharma ads. Interesting. What percentage of the total ads do they occupy? Do you think they have to pay more for those same ad buys during election years when political ads are taking up more of the advertising slots? See Part 8 for more on this intriguing topic.

News Hounds From the Old Days

Scurrilous Commentary by Fred Reed

God's Knights of the Pen and Bottle: The Noble Reporter in His Splendor

Posted on February 8, 2018 by Fred Reed

Check out this article from a retired Vietnam war correspondent: https://fredoneverything.org/gods-knights-of-the-pen-and-bottle-the-noble-reporter-in-his-splendor/

Read closely, dig the prose and think about how it is for these people covering public/wartime events. Pay special attention to how the TV crews approach reporting and how the print reporters think ill of them. "It was only later that we got prissy delicates who probably drank designer water in fern bars instead of sour mash."

Think about this depiction of the old days in contrast to our discussion and chapter on "transactional journalism." There used to be truth seekers, as opposed to favor traders. The part about the photographers is especially good: "Every photographer will carefully frame out the other newsmen, giving the salable impression that he alone was out there in no man's land."

These journalists seemed to be in it for the grit and the experience. They weren't going to come back and sugar coat things because they had some arrangement with people in power.

This one line kind of says it all: "If a reporter thought he saw glimmerings of human decency in a politician or a lawyer, he would have his eyes checked."

If there are reporters and journalists like this out there in the world today, let's find them and make sure they're able to continue reporting.

Part 8 – Advertising and the Political Cycle

Political advertising and political races in America are a unique animal. The U.S. is the world leader in media, persuasion, advertising, technology and a host of other industries (wink, wink – defense). These first four, however, are important when it comes to election cycles.

Most people are not going to be happy with this next assertion, but it's true and transparent once you put your eyes and thoughts onto it.

Politicians that play "big league" ball are elected or re-elected every 2 to 4 years. It's like the Winter/Summer Olympics schedule. Every two years there are congressional elections, and every four years there are presidential and congressional elections. State legislature and governorship elections are sprinkled in along similar 2 and 4 year cycles, but they don't always coincide with the national congressional or presidential elections.

So why is the two and four year cycle important? For network news, it's a cash cow. Between these two and four stints, politicians are typically legislating and pontificating. True, there is some validity to the idea that modern politicians are in perpetual campaign mode. However, every two to four years, the shite goes down. They have to be re-elected or have their propositions and measures approved or abolished. And, viewers tune into news much more often when there's a political race going on that could affect their lives, pocketbooks or political egos.

How do politicians get their messages out? Via the news media. They come onto the shows in prime time, and the news media follows them around at speeches, town halls and various staged events. The mainstream media has special access to these politicians, as well. Not every blogger and YouTuber gets access to the press rooms and press pools. The politicians become the media product (or sometimes entertainment product) in a sense. Having access to them, their ideas and their charades gives the news media instant content for their programming – content that viewers have historically eaten up by the trough full.

And, how does the news media make money? Political ad buys that occur on a 2-4 year basis. Get it? It's a symbiotic relationship.

Here's a diagram of how the money flows:

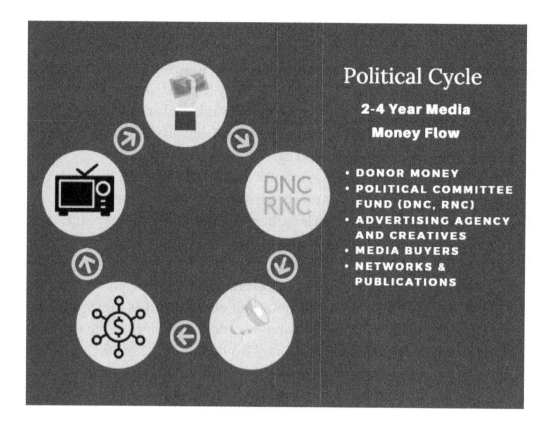

In a way, the networks are taking money from the candidates as a form of payment for exposing the candidates (favorably and sometimes unfavorably. Remember, most in the political scene now consider staying in the headlines more important than positive or negative coverage. Any coverage is good coverage. The candidate becomes the news product. Simultaneously, the candidate's advertising uses tested persuasion techniques (mostly fear-based, by the way) directly on the viewing public.

If the candidate is elected, he or she builds up a war chest for the party, and then the cycle starts all over again two years later.

If you learn anything from this course, this might be the most important lesson. The news media and political interests are linked up in a super cozy relationship. The nightly news wouldn't exist without mid-term and full-term elections. News teams get special access to politicians and other important consultants and pundits every two to four years, because it helps the network/blog/podcast/newspaper sell ads in their publication. In turn, they receive large cash infusions from the party PR, publicity, promotion and re-election budgets. This is huge business. The news organizations at NBC, ABC, CBS, CNN, FOX and all the other little ones couldn't exist without this relationship. Journalists get access. Politicians, PACs, and parties pay to play via ad buys. It's that crazy simple.

We're going to complicate it a bit, however. When you have a large political race, such as a presidential election, *where* the actual advertising dollars are spent becomes an issue that doesn't get much attention. I want you to consider two states:

- New York
- California

Those states have voted overwhelmingly for the Democratic presidential nominee since the elections of Ronald Reagan in 1980 and 1984. Both states have voted blue (donkey) ever since, and the numbers have become out of balance. There have been no close races for the red (elephant) challenger in those states since 1984. It's been a clean run for 34 years.

Then, I'd like you to consider four other states:

- Michigan
- Pennsylvania
- Ohio
- Florida

Michigan voted for a Republican candidate by a fairly comfortable margin in 1988 (George H.W. Bush) – about an 8% delta. Then they voted solidly democrat all the way through to Obama's second term in 2012. Bill Clinton won by healthy margins in the 1990s. Voting was tight, with differentials of 3% to 5% in the elections of 2000 and 2004, where George

W. Bush won those elections (Republican). The state of Michigan voted for Barack Obama by comfortable margins in 2008 and 2012. In 2016, the state voted for Trump by a slim margin – a tad higher than ¼% point! Now that's a tight race.

Pennsylvania and Ohio have similar stats. Florida is a doozy. Read up on the 2000 election if you want to learn more about how tight that one was. What's common is that all four states can be up for grabs in any presidential election, *unless* the candidate is beloved or presides over wonderful economic times like a Reagan, Clinton or Obama.

Now compare that slim Michigan margin of ¼% in the Donald Trump election to the percentage of margin in California. In 2016, the percent delta for Hillary Clinton was an overwhelming 30%. There was not chance for Trump in California. Just like there was probably no chance for Hillary Clinton in Tennessee. Donald Trump won the vote there by a 26% margin – 60.7% to 34.7%. That's a landslide.

So, now we have to ask ourselves if we're managing the ad budgets for Hillary and Donald in the 2016 race – Where do we spend our money?

Answers: Donald, don't spend a dime in California or New York (and some other places like Illinois). Spend your money wisely in Michigan, Pennsylvania, Ohio and Florida – all states that he won. Hillary, don't spend a dime in California or New York (and Illinois). Spend it all in the "swing states."

In California we saw very few presidential political ads for either candidate. The swing states were peppered with ads on all media, morning, noon and night.

So, there's an economic distortion force at work. All these huge TV concerns (most network news is broadcast out of New York, and Hollywood drives much of the entertainment news) and major publications like The New York Times, The San Francisco Chronicle and The Los Angeles Times get no share of that big juicy money pie. Media outlets in the swing states get rich while California, New York and Illinois starve. It's a weird thing. You might even say it's broken in some way, especially when a race is tight. But there's a price to pay when you're a state that doesn't have a balanced electorate. The news networks and media publications would love it if every state had a slim voting margin like Michigan's ¼%. The money would flow evenly to everyone, more might be spent, and dollars wouldn't concentrate in a half dozen states.

This brings us to conspiracy talk. If you think about presidential elections from the perspective of the media, it gets interesting. Presidential elections gather the most eyeballs for TVs, blogs, newspapers, podcasts, and YouTube channels. It's *the* American event for whipping up emotions, pulling apart families, pitting co-workers against each other, generating millions of annoying Facebook posts and more. It's where the big bucks are, and it's where the news media makes a huge portion of their revenues. They make some during the midterm elections, but presidential elections bring in the lion's share of the money.

Ask yourself: What would be the biggest motivation for these networks, blogs, platforms (AdWords/Facebook), podcasts, news aggregators (Huffington Post and The Drudge Report) and traditional publishers?

Answer: ***The illusion of a close race!***

So here's the deal. We live in a data-driven society, where polls and pollsters are supposed to be super-accurate in the political sphere. There are even shows, news segments and interviews with polling experts that happen during presidential elections. That's how big of a "science" it is.

Why then, did nobody predict Clinton/George H.W. Bush/Reagan/Obama landslides? Well, not nobody, but if you watched the network news coverage, you'd see a whole lot of noise about how close the races were.

There are a few of the significant polls that political types track:

- Rasmussen
- WSJ/NBC
- CNN
- Pew
- Quinnipiac
- Marist

- Mason-Dixon
- Reuters/Ipsos
- Economist/YouGov
- Gallup
- Monmouth
- Fox News

The following link shows you aggregate polls on the latest political races: https://realclearpolitics.com/epolls/latest_polls/

There are people that are actually paid to keep tabs on these polls day to day, if you can believe it.

Next, look at the 2000 election that ended up going crazy in Florida when George W. Bush defeated Al Gore, of climate change fame. That was an actual close race that came down to ballot recounts. The money, ads and influence kept Americans engaged with the news cycle much further past their previous tolerance levels.

2016 Election Poll Analysis
Read the following analysis to understand more about the mistakes made by the polls and the pundits in the 2016 election.

http://bit.ly/2r5iqTN

AAPOR
2016
POLL ANALYSIS

Did the Media Turn On Trump?

Given the diagram at the beginning of Part 8 and the way the system works, you have to ask yourself why the media (except for Fox) turned on

Donald Trump from the outset of his campaign? Or, maybe he turned on himself.

Remember, when he was running Celebrity Apprentice, there were no claims about sex scandals, Islamophobia, homophobia, Xenophobia, etc. He was beaten in the press before he could even open up the campaign war chest.

Answer: He broke the advertising model we've been discussing. He grabbed headlines in the very publications and broadcasts that he'd have to pay via advertising with a few simple Tweets. He dominated the news cycle without paying into the old game. He owned the attention of millions in the very outlets he, traditionally, should have been advertising in! It was either a crazy accident or a stroke of brilliance.

We can let the crazy partisans figure that one out. Yet it remains a fact. Trump didn't have to spend nearly as much as Clinton because much of his coverage (though negative) was free – the best kind of PR available.

Trump wrote about this kind of strategy in *Art of the Deal* (1987). He used it to great effect when promoting his TV shows, as well. You simply gain exposure and your message spreads with positive and/or negative coverage. Hollywood has a similar adage about actors. It goes something like this: *If they're not talking about you (good or bad), you're washed up or don't exist.* It's why coverage for actors in *US Weekly, The National Enquirer, People Magazine, The Star* and similar magazines is so important for keeping careers in the spotlight. Actors used to sue those magazines for defamation and slander, but they now curry favor from the publications in order to keep their work and their personages in the public eye. The Kardashians perform these public spectacles expertly. In a way, they use the same approach as Trump. Grab headlines no matter what the consequence, and your personality and ideas will always be relevant.

An Analogy: Network News as the Favorite Team

Everybody loves their favorite sports team. New England Patriots fans are wild about Tom Brady and the Pats. Canadians love their hockey teams. Most Southern Californians love either the Lakers, the USC Trojans or the UCLA Bruins or some combination thereof. People are absolutely passionate about their sports teams. They'll wear clothing to support them, scream at the TV when they get scored on, attend watch parties with like-minded fans, and travel far and wide to catch a game in person. They also follow their favorite players with incredible fervor and research.

I'm going to pose an analogy. The network news channels watched by older generations are almost like teams, with familiar players that people feel comfortable watching. They also trumpet familiar themes, positions and issues that their watchers align with. People know how the offense works and how the defense plays. They're familiar with the hosts' argumentative style and approach.

Geraldo Rivera is a certain way on camera. Some people like where he's coming from. Chris Matthews has followers, as does Rachel Maddow. Tucker Carlson and Sean Hannity have their fans. The cable news networks are where the bulk of the viewers huddle, Fox and CNN being the front runners. Older demographics watch network news (ABC, CBS, NBC) - the channels they grew up with and trust.

If we look at the ratings (the number of viewers watching a program on a given night - quantified as a ratings number devised by TVNewser), we see a close 50/50 split in viewership along conservative/liberal lines. It's similar to the electorate's split between Republicans and Democrats.

Here are the cable news ratings from Adweek TVNewser for a Monday night in February, 2018:

Scoreboard: Monday, Feb. 5

f Share   Tweet   More

By A.J. Katz on Feb. 6, 2018 - 4:32 PM   Comment

25-54 demographic (Live +SD)

- Total day: FNC: 431 | CNN: 268 | MSNBC: 279 | HLN: 83
- Prime time: FNC: 743 | CNN: 404 | MSNBC: 554 | HLN: 118

	4p:	5p:	6p:	7p:	8p:	9p:	10p:	11p:
FNC	Cavuto: 322	Five: 512	Baier: 551	MacCallum: 518	Carlson: 749	Hannity: 850	Ingraham: 629	Bream: 425
CNN	Tapper: 253	Blitzer: 279	Blitzer: 315	Burnett: 395	Cooper: 413	Cooper: 431	Tonight: 368	Tonight: 284
MSNBC	Wallace: 239	MTPDaily: 257	Melber: 348	Matthews: 355	Hayes: 429	Maddow: 739	O'Donnell: 493	Wlms: 347
HLN	Michaela: 32	Cupp: 21	Banfield: 27	Banfield: 52	Files: 83	Files: 105	Files: 166	Files: 204

Total Viewers (Live +SD)

- Total day: FNC: 2.035 | CNN: 785 | MSNBC: 1.337 | HLN: 243
- Primetime: FNC: 3.490 | CNN: 1.127 | MSNBC: 2.558 | HLN: 352

As you can see, the channel that's considered very conservative or Republican, Fox News Channel (FNC), has a fairly big lead in most time slots. MSNBC, which is considered very liberal or Democratic, is the yang to Fox's yin. CNN is considered liberal/Democratic. HLN is a spin-off from CNN and is owned by the same parent company. While Fox appears to lead the numbers game, generally most news watchers are watching liberal or Democratic presentations of the news. None of this, of course, considers the way many of us get our news – the Internet, Twitter, Facebook, LinkedIn and email from friends. The broadcast and cable concerns have audiences on the Internet, as well, with, print, audio (podcast) and video. They just don't have the kind of dominance they have on the old-fashioned TV set.

Broadcast network news is a different animal. Traditionally, the medium has not been so heavy handed with commentary and opinion, although that's changing. What's worked for the cable channels is division and argument on camera. This could be an outgrowth of the Jerry Springer trend that happened in the 1990's on daytime TV. Springer was known for getting fiercely combative guests onto his show and letting them have at it. He was a provocateur of sorts. Take a spin through YouTube and see some of that funny stuff.

The broadcast networks, however, rely more on straight reporting and less on guest-guest or anchor-guest arguments. It's a sober spin through the news of the day.

Here are the ratings numbers for network news:

ABC's World News Tonight with **David Muir** was the most-watched evening newscast last week, and, once again, the only broadcast to see year-over-year growth.

NBC Nightly News with **Lester Holt** continued to lead among younger viewers with a +6 percent lead on World News Tonight.

Compared to the same week last year ABC was up +3 percent in viewers, but

down -4 percent in the A25-54 demo; Nightly News was down -4 percent in viewers and down -9 percent in the demo. The CBS Evening News with **Jeff Glor** was down -6 percent in viewers and down -8 percent in the demo compared to the same week last year.

Numbers for the week of Jan. 29, 2018:

	ABC	NBC	CBS
• Total Viewers:	9,267,000	8,759,000	6,869,000
• A25-54:	1,914,000	2,030,000	1,447,000

For whatever reason, Adweek (the originator of these numbers) has different metrics . They're going by actual viewers in the case of the broadcast networks, but they have ratings numbers for the cable networks.

You'll see Adweek focuses on the 24-54 year old demographic. Why? Advertising, of course.

People in that age range have the most interest in news and the most money to spend on the kinds of things advertised on news shows. The viewership is both young and impressionable (to branding efforts – think cars and insurance), and old and making decisions about foods and healthcare. That's the sweet spot. Adweek knows this. They're the pros. It's their business to advise advertisers.

Look at those broadcast numbers again. What stands out? The 25-54 demo is pretty small compared to the overall numbers. Do you think the rest is people under 25? Doubtful! The rest of broadcast news viewers are over 54. They grew up watching those networks and didn't take to cable. Or maybe they do both.

In any event the 55+ crowd is the perfect audience for all those pharma ads we talked about. These people are coming up against cancer, acid reflux, impotence, heart disease and all that. They're highly likely to have a conversation with their doctor about Humira.

Exercise: Ask 4 people – parents or older – what their favorite news network is and why they watch it. Think CNN, Fox, MSNBC, ABC, NBC and CBS here. I don't think many are going to say RT (Russia Today). You'll probably see a split which looks something like this:

Fox News	CNN
	CBS
	ABC
	NBC
	MSNBC

The conservatives will be watching the left column, and the liberals will be watching the right. This doesn't look "fair and balanced" at a glance, but a large portion – maybe 40% of the viewers are watching Fox News, so there's definitely a split that reflects the political electorate in this country.

Now, go to Google Trends and pick a topic at the top of the list that interests you. Google Trends shows you the topics that people are searching in the news and on the web in any given day. You can do the same by looking at Twitter trends. Beware, there are lots of stupid things going on in these trend feeds. Be prepared for a heavy dose of Kardashians and other filth. If you go to the menu on the left, you can sort by trending searches.

Now email a conservative friend or family member about that particular topic, asking them for their thoughts. Do the same with a liberal friend or family member. It doesn't necessarily have to be a controversial topic, but it should be exposed enough to have reached most of the country via headlines "above the fold."

Bring in your findings, and we'll discuss. Hopefully, we'll get some fun stuff back. I'm guessing we'll get some humor, rage, insights and quirkiness.

Part 9 – Bringing it All Together

Think about all of this with a comparison of two people. Ted and Steve are recent college graduates. They attended respectable schools and graduated with 3.5 grade point averages, some party skills, and a slightly better understanding of females than their former high school selves.

Ted goes to work for a technology company, where a lot of the older programmers are faithful readers and watchers of traditional media. They watch NBC, read the LA Times and occasionally dabble in the Financial Times or the Wall Street Journal. Ted is happy to fit in with his new peer group. The older programmers have a great time spouting off about politics and public figures based on their consumption of traditional/generic news. Their zingers and one-liners mimic the talking points presented by mainstream media. They are funny to larger groups of people, because they feed the same lines given to them by the media back to their friends and associates, but with added irony, sarcasm and biting commentary. They mix common sense with the staid storylines of the news and come up with some fun banter.

This group also chides each other about diet choices based on mainstream (often conflicting) research about everything from caffeine and coffee to diet fads and pharmaceuticals.

They are a very busy bunch, so they don't have much time to dive deep into topics. They compile "headline information" into their heads. Their understanding of world events is good enough to produce interesting recall and mixing of subject matter. This produces humor and insights similar to what many of the late-night TV comedians can muster.

Ted drinks energy drinks to keep up with his fast-paced work life and orders out for meals quite often, thinking that he's saving time. At his home, he has a TV in his kitchen, one in his bathroom near the mirror next to the shower, and a big 4K screen with an Xbox in his living room. His morning weekday routine includes powering up all the TVs so the day's news can follow him around his house. By the time he leaves for work, his brain has been filled with all the news (what's been decided as important by a very small group of *New York Times* and network news producers/publishers) of the day. Some of the news he consumes comes via social networks like Facebook and LinkedIn.

Steve took a course like the one you just completed. He's not a journalist, a marketing expert or a media analyst, but he has a critical eye on all the stories he's being fed by the media and some of the potential sources of these stories. He knows that the news media is built on a tradition of pay-to-play PR and coverage that's dominated by sports teams, large businesses, powerful entertainment interests, and well-organized organizations (including NGOs and government agencies).

He works at an e-Commerce company that sells supplements via Amazon.com. On weekdays, Steve wakes up and exercises. He tries to meditate in the early morning hours, too. Since he knows what some of the health risks are for media consumption, he carefully plans his avoidance of morning messages and the "cloud of confusion" offered up by typical media outlets.

He visits a curated list of news sites from time to time, but he doesn't consume media on a daily basis. The list of sites and YouTube channels he visits are a carefully selected cross-section of conservative, liberal, libertarian, alternative, and conspiratorial resources. When he does consume news, he's looking for patterns and themes that bounce around amongst all these types of outlets. When big, breaking news hits, he waits at least 2 days for the dust to settle, knowing that first hour and first day accounts of tragic incidents usually promote a lot of misinformation. He actively tries to stay away from social media and forces himself to avoid aligning with any "team" like right-wingers, leftists, globalists, environmentalists or statists. He shares his voting habits and political opinions with very few people. He identifies and understands product/philosophy/ideology pitches that are embedded within popular culture/media (movies, sports, sit-coms, news analysis, consumer surveys, etc.).

Ted becomes easily outraged by stories he sees in the news. A report on the toxicity of certain coffee beans can easily set him off, as can a story about the latest gun attack. He personalizes a lot of the feelings in the stories and even adopts some of the cadences and seriousness of the on-air talent that convey the stories. When news is discussed by his friends on social media sites, he can become even more agitated. He feels a need to set people straight with his particular point of view. He does, however, gain some comfort from commiserating with people on social media. His friends share many of his views.

Ted takes a statin for hypertension and "bad" cholesterol levels. This statin is advertised heavily on major news networks. When his doctor recommended he go on a heart health control drug, he knew this particular one by name. He drinks beer advertised on Sunday NFL broadcasts and has a home security system that he bought from a 1-800 number featured on a nightly news advertisement.

Steve recognizes that he's not able to make heads or tails of any network-promoted report on coffee, fat, cholesterol, alcohol, marijuana or any other journalistically-obsessed-on topic. He concedes that he doesn't know a lot about how the government conducts foreign wars and international intercessions. He tries to keep an eye on his neighborhood, his business relationships, his friends and his family. e

Steve ignores most political topics that arise in social situations. Ted feeds off of and into those same types of exchanges.

Who is more calm, happy and well adjusted? Ted or Steve? What would the news media have you believe? Is an informed person (one informed by settled facts) happier than one who doesn't know as much information? Is more information detrimental? Which one of these guys makes better decisions about the things that affect their lives?

Social Media Burnout? What's Next? Some Predictions.

As of this writing, you're seeing many elements of society and the government pushing back heavily on social media networks and ad platforms like Facebook and Google.

The news is full of stories about:

- Bullying
- Unnecessary competition and showiness
- Fake ads
- Russian collusion to overturn our elections
- Troll farms influencing us
- Bots clicking on ads
- Murders on Instagram
- Weird death scenes on YouTube
- Busted YouTube celebrities for the last two

It's just endless. Here are some predictions about what comes next. Take them with a grain of salt.

#1: The government and corporate America will eventually get on the same page and recognize that we're experiencing a huge productivity drain on the economy. People are dorking around at work. That's no bueno. People are running their Etsy businesses from their work cubicles, and that's got to stop. You're either working for the man or working for yourself. What kinds of measures will evolve is anyone's guess.

#2: People will burn out on social networks. I think we're already seeing this. Younger generations prefer one-to-one messaging, and adults have been through the ringer, reading their friends' rants on Facebook – friends who, by the way, are not Poli Sci professors from the world's leading colleges.

#Counter argument to #2: Did people burnout from TV? All media tends to be additive. Maybe it could come crashing down at some point. The war between the parties and ideologues could speed this up. I'd describe this as lots of 'death of a thousand cuts' wars between the Soros/Media Matters crowd and the Koch brothers/Murdoch crowd. A lot of that influence has produced events that have been very confusing for the American public, like: fake protests in the streets, Antifa, Black Lives Matter, anti-globalists, globalists, anarchists, and the occupy Wall Street movement of years ago (Seattle). Maybe all this division will cripple social media platforms. After all, with past media, you could not argue with the radio receiver, the front pages, the TV or the movie screen. You didn't prank the local newscaster with a F* her by the P* interruption. It's now a two-way media street. We'll see.

#3: Social networks will turn into commerce platforms primarily. This is already going on. The only non-political, non-offensive stuff on these networks is really great personal productions, funny t-shirts, health and diet stuff, consumer electronics and associated gadgets. Expect this trend to continue as the social networks censor news and people don't trust the news feeds.

#4: Smear merchants and political issue brigades will continue to buy your eyeballs via Google Ads, SEO, social media ads, Reddit threads, comment threads on popular media sites and more. More of the same. More confusion. More smoke.

#5: "Data cowboys" William Gibson's *Neuromancer* will significantly disrupt the world networks. There will be warfare on the net like we've never seen. Again, this could already be in progress (think STUXNET).

#6: The U.S. government or something like the EU will attempt to regulate speech and commerce online. They'll try to make it "safe" for advertising and economics again. Remember, the Internet started as an academic exchange of information. Then it turned commerce. Then it turned political/social cesspool plus commerce. This should end up with heavy pressure on Facebook and Google, which some people consider the internet. Those will be the safe places to advertise and sell. Some other part of the network will be relegated to Wild West, unregulated stuff. Somewhere like Reddit. . . segmentation of the net into safe and dark.

Questions Moving Forward

With all the information and theories uncovered in this course, there are some pertinent questions to ask:

- How will your understanding of the media shape how you view the world and your role in it?
- Can you be a healthier person by changing the way you approach news and think about how it's put together?
- How can you lead a better life knowing what you know and with the ability to see things as they are?
- Are you able to recognize when you're up against information that has dubious intent?
- How can you structure your life and your media consumption habits in order to gain maximum health, clarity, purpose and insight?

RECOMMENDED TEXTS & ARTICLES

- _Amusing Ourselves to Death_, Neil Postman
- _The Smear: How Shady Political Operatives and Fake News Control What You See, What You Think, and How You Vote_, Sharyl Attkisson
- _Persuasion in Society_, Herbert W. Simons and Jean G. Jones
- _Win Bigly_: Persuasion in a World Where Facts Don't Matter,

Scott Adams
- *Sports in America*, James A. Michener
- *The New Confessions of an Economic Hit Man*, John Perkins
- *Influence*, Robert Cialdini, Ph. D.
- *Pre-Suasion*, Robert Cialdini, Ph. D.
- *Truth in Digital Advertising* – Scientific American, David Pogue, article
- *Advertising Click-Bot Fraud* – Oxford BioChonometrics study
- *The 2016 Election and the Demise of Journalistic Standards*, Imprimis Hillsdale College, Michael Goodwin, article

ABOUT THE AUTHOR

I'm a professional marketer and journalist with an M.A. in print journalism from the University of Southern California, a B.A. in history from UC Berkeley, and 23 years of marketing, reporting and publishing experience. My companies, QualityWriter and Synapse Services Co., help businesses tell their stories via digital marketing and content development strategies. I'm also the author of McGraw-Hill's best-selling eBay marketing book *The 7 Essential Steps to Successful eBay Marketing*.

I wrote *Media Collusion* and developed the companion course to teach my kids about the media and how it influences their lives. I have two sons, aged 15 and 13 at the time of this writing, and one daughter who's now 10. It's my hope that I can teach other college prep students the same course material so they too can better navigate this challenging media landscape and digital advertising world.

I'll share my views up front, so you can make any assumptions you require and temper your understandings about the materials within by knowing the person behind the words. I don't profess to be an expert on all the topics covered in this book, but I've worked with the experts, practiced much of what's described professionally, and have a long, complex relationship with advertising and the media.

I grew up in Orange County, California, son of an U.S. Air Force spy pilot, software publishing entrepreneur and computer programmer father and a graphic designer and fine artist mother. I was home sick the day Ronald Reagan was shot and soaked up every minute of the news reporting. I really liked the guy and, as believer in the adage, *"The chief business of the American people is business,"* attributed to Calvin Coolidge the 30th U.S. President, fully appreciated his tax strategies, as well as JFK's very similar pro-growth policies. My general sense is that if you give people enough prosperity, they'll figure out the other issues within their communities, as free people. Too much legislation mucks up the gears of progress.

I've voted for Democrats, Libertarians and Republicans, and I'm currently registered as an Independent voter. I've been registered as a Libertarian and a Republican in the past. My first presidential vote (while in college) was for Michael Dukakis, the Democrat candidate. He promised to allow college grads into a program that would offer mortgage down payments at 3% of the total. That was my first taste of the bitter campaign season medicine so common in U.S. politics – candidates make outlandish campaign-trail claims, only to walk them back later. Everybody does it. Only the young and naïve fall for it.

My media and advertising/marketing backgrounds are important. I understand who journalists are from inside, personal experience. My colleagues and fellow Masters candidates at USC's School of Journalism were predominantly activists of liberal persuasion, and they felt it their duty to write and report in order to advance specific policies and cultural imperatives. That's the reality for the "feet on the street." I'm cynical in that sense, and I abandoned a full-time career in the news business in favor of marketing, which you'll learn is just another form of the news (from the pages of this book). The other important players in the media game (advertisers, publishers and policy influencers) are more complicated animals. There are families, companies, politicians, non-profit organizations and government entities that all heavily influence the news. We'll go deep into this system within these pages.

The book is written with the U.S. media and advertising industries as a backdrop, however the material should be applicable to all kinds of countries and cultures around the globe. U.S. politics, culture and popular media have traveled far and wide over the past century. The lessons should be recognizable and transferable to a wide audience of international readers.

One thing I'd like to avoid in these pages and in the course material is political divisiveness. We all have our views, and there's certainly a vested interest by the powers that be in an "us vs. them" game. I'll keep the examples in this text balanced, so we can all get a laugh out of the games that all parties play without getting bogged down in opinion, dogma or general indignation.

This book is not about politics. It's about the media powers in play and how the game is played. Once you understand how it works, you may end up chucking the whole notion of "staying informed" and go pursue other endeavors. I've certainly put myself on a news diet. I spend my limited thoughts (by age!) and emotions on oil painting, gourmet cooking, enjoying my family, neighborhood and friends, and getting in the odd surf session or hockey game.

ACKNOWLEDGMENTS

Thanks to all the people who have listened to me drone on about these issues and dream about writing a book. Special thanks to Jim Thrasher and Steve Reed who contributed to this first edition.

Even more monumental appreciation goes out to John C. Dvorak and Adam Curry of *The No Agenda Show*. Their podcast inspires professionals across all industries to question authority, examine things closely, pay attention to words, and call BS on the players who manipulate the public.

INDEX

Made in the USA
Columbia, SC
08 June 2018